Tomasz J. Kowalski

Albatros D.I–D.Va
Legendary fighter

KAGERO

Contents

Albatros D.I–D.Va Legendary fighter • Tomasz J. Kowalski
First edition • LUBLIN 2010

ISBN: 978-83-61220-73-2

Translation: Rafał Iwiński
Proof reading: Piotr Kolasa
Photos: Unless credited otherwise, all photographs in this book are from the Author's collection
Colour plates: Janusz Światłoń
DTP: Małgorzata Dudziak, KAGERO STUDIO

Oficyna Wydawnicza KAGERO
www.kagero.pl • e-mail: kagero@kagero.pl, marketing@kagero.pl

Editorial office, Marketing, Distribution:
KAGERO Publishing Sp. z o.o., ul. Mełgiewska 9F, 20-209 Lublin
tel.: (+48) 081 749 20 20, tel./fax (+48) 081 749 11 81, www.kagero.pl

One of the Albatros D.I prototypes. Cleary visible unbalanced elevator and vertical exhaust pipe.

"The Albatros D-III popularly known as *De-drei* is a sleek single-seat biplane fighter armed with two machine guns shooting through the propeller arc. It goes up like a balloon, while its speed at full throttle is up to one hundred seventy kilometers per hour.

'Be careful when taking off: it has a very sensitive rudder!'

Then there is just the engine check to complete, "remove chocks" and I am off taxing for takeoff, I raise my hand to indicate I am ready, I get the go-ahead flag signal and push the throttle lever to full rpm. The aircraft sets off like a racehorse immediately gaining speed, just begging to get airborne. Wheels clear the ground – I am airborne! I had not even had time to 'be careful when taking off,' the plane just took me away to the skies, carrying as it goes – and it can go!

I try to use ailerons, then the elevator, eventually the rudder; the stick and rudder bar move lightly, they offer virtuallty no resistance, while the plane rolls to the sides, climbs and dives, turns smoothly and lightly, without any delay; it is running fine, agile and maneuverable like a swallow. I like the *De-drei* immensely."

The way Janusz Meissner described the Albatros D.III in his book *Jak dziś pamiętam*[1] shows the pilot's fascination with the plane. It also proves the merits of the design that originated in 1910 from a German aviation factory Albatros Werke G.m.b.H. Its main office

was in Johannisthal, Berlin, while its O.A.W branch was in Schneidemühl (present-day Piła). From 1916 onwards, Albatros fighters presented a large percentage of fighter planes in combat units, with many aces having flown them. Therefore it is worth to look closely at the history of that aircraft type.

The Albatros fighters played an important role in the aerial warfare of the Great War. They were the workhorse of the German air service from the autumn of 1916 to the summer of 1918. During that time the Albatros had become the most popular fighter type not only in German service, but also in Turkish, Austro-Hungarian and Bulgarian units-, quite contrary to common beliefs that the Fokkers, especially the Dr.I and D.VII models, were the quintessential World War I fighters. The Fokker may owe its claim to fame to Hollywood productions that immortalized its image as "the" German fighter, or perhaps it was the result of a vigorous marketing campaign launched by Anthony Fokker himself.

Whatever the case may be, it is an undisputed fact that over 350 German fighter pilots earned the 'ace' title – scored five or more kills – flying the Albatros and 29 of them went on to receive the highest German decoration – the Pour Le Meritte (Blue Max).

For those reasons the history of a design that was born at the German Albatros Werke G.m.b.H. deserves a closer look.

The fuselage of an early Albatros D.I (serial probably 384/16) shot down on March 21, 1917, by Lt. Pickthorn from RFC's No. 32 Squadron. The grey green (Brunschwig gren) Albatros had been piloted by Prince Friedrich-Karl von Preussen who took it over from Jasta 2's Lt d R. Dieter Collin (scored two victories in this aeroplane). The Prince ordered to remove Collin's personal insignia and paint an emblem of the Hussar Regiment he had served in.

The Graceful Fighter

Any war is the time when military hardware is developed and ideas how to use it in the field evolve. The Great War was the time when military aviation boomed rapidly. Very early on it became clear that there was no such thing as a universal aircraft that could meet the ever growing needs of reconnaissance, bombing raids, liaison, directing artillery fire and, finally, engaging enemy planes in the air.

Makeshift adaptations of available machines for fighter duties were insufficient. By the end of 1915, a concept had developed that fighters should be able to fire machine guns in the direction of flight. The British and French tried to solve the issue by introducing pusher designs, i.e. the aircraft with the engines installed behind the crew cockpits, so that the rotating propeller would not interfere with shooting.

Another option was to conceive a device for front-engine planes that would prevent the rounds from ripping through the propeller. A Frenchman named Roland Garros applied a deflector – propeller cover pads deflecting the fired rounds. Having examined the wreckage of Roland Garros' Morane, Anthony Fokker, a Dutchman working in Germany, built a synchronizer – a mechanical instrument preventing firing a round if a propeller blade was in front of a gun muzzle. He fitted the synchronizer in a single-seat monoplane that was based on the French Mo-rane H – and so the formidable Fokker E.I was born. When it reached the frontline it gave the Germans air superiority. The first Fokker victory was won by Max Immelman on August 1, 1915, followed by Oswald Böelcke on August 19. Both pilots served in Feldflieger Abteilung 62. Twenty six Fokkers scattered over various units inflicted heavy losses on the Allies and forced them to commence group flying as a defensive measure. The Allies responded with the Nieuport[2] 11C1 that hit the frontlines in January 1916. This fast and maneuverable sesquiplane became more effective than the "Fokker Scourge" as it was continuously undergoing improvements. Eventually the Allies won air superiority.

The Fokker and Nieuport laid the foundations for all future fighter designs. A fighter aircraft was to be a small, maneuverable and fast single-seater with a high climb-rate, armed with at least one machine gun firing through the propeller arc. Since biplanes and sesquiplanes offered more maneuverability at that time, such design layouts were preferred when building fighters. There were of course exceptions to the rule, but as the saying goes they just proved the rule.

Losing air superiority forced Germany to design new fighters. On August 31, 1916, General Ernst von Hoeppner commanding German air forces commented: "Performance offered by a monoplane powered by a 118-kW engine after fitting the second machine gun is the peak of its potential. D-class biplanes entering service offer better maneuverability, climb-rate and speed in level flight. They must supersede the E class."

Inspired by Oswald Böelcke, a process of forming dedicated Jagdstaffeln units began (with the first being set up in August 1916) to replace the ad hoc created Kampfeinsitzer Komando (KEK). The primary requirement was to secure proper equipment. The poorly designed Fokker D.I was withdrawn from frontline service rather quickly as the sloppy workmanship used in its manufacturing became apparent. All the aircraft were reassigned to training duties. Although D.Is and D.IIs from Roland works and D.IIs and D.IIIs from Halberstadt turned out to be quite good, they did not improve the situation much.

The Albatros plant produced 5 prototypes D.344-348/16. One of them – the 256 – was used for static tests, while the 2759 was test flown by Ernst von Lössi. On June 17, he achieved the following climb rates: 1000 m in 4 min., 2000 m in 8 min. 3000 m in 14 min. When put into serial production the Albatros would climb to 4000 m in 30 minutes.

In June 1916 Albatros Werke G.m.b.H. received an order for twelve prototypes (serials D.381-D.392/16) of single-seat fighter biplanes. Under the terms of the contract the aircraft were to be powered by the 118-kW (160-hp) in-line, liquid cooled Mercedes D.III engine.

Although it is difficult to retrace the work done by a team headed by engineers Robert Thellen[3], Rudolf Schubert and Gnaedig, we know that the **Albatros D.I (L.15)**[4] had been built in a short time (according to R.L. Rimel, in 13 days). After tests at Ideflieg it was approved by the Zentral Abname Kommision (Central Acceptance Commision) as hardware fit for military units.

The old mantra "if it looks good, it'll fly good" certainly applies to the Albatros design. The designers worked hard on aerodynamic qualities of the wooden, semi-monocoque, oval cross-section fuselage that in its front part smoothly transformed into a large cowling covering the propeller hub. The middle and aft sections of the fuselage were flat while its upper and bottom parts were gently rounded. The engine was almost completely embedded in the fuselage, only cylinder heads, the cooling liquid tank and exhaust pipes with a manifold protruded beyond its lines. The fuselage, together with plywood-skinned vertical stabilizer and stabilizing fin constituted a single airframe element. The engine was accessible through removable metal panels. In front of the cockpit, at either side of the fuselage, were Windhoff radiators.

The plane was fitted with two-spar, rectangular wings with rounded wooden wingtips. The Albatros prototype was designed with canvas-covered wings of uneven depth: the upper had 1.75 m while the lower 1.60 m. Moreover, the latter had a slightly shorter wingspan than the former. In order to increase visibility a semi-circular cut-out was made in the upper wing mid-section. The lower wing was

Lt. Manfred von Richtchofen's Albatros D.II D.481/16 with white spinner and nose band. The four Jasta 2 pilots standing in front of the fighter are, from left to right: Stephan Kirmaier, Hans Immelman, Manfred von Richtchofen (in a sweater), Hans Wortman.

Albatros D.I 423/16 in plain varnish fuselage and fin (natural plywood color with a varnish finish).

Albatros D.I 497/16 in stained and varnish fuselage and fin, terrain camouflage on upper surfaces with pale blue lower wing surfaces and tailplane. The Aircraft was used in Jasta 2.

An early example of the Albatros D.III with a centrally mounted Teves und Braun radiator.

attached to the fuselage while the upper was based on an inverted V-shaped, steel tube pyramid. The wing cell was composed of two parallel struts with teardrop cross-section, braced with steel wire strings.

The two-strut undercarriage had a fixed axle embedded in a cowling and was fitted with a rubber string shock absorber. The wooden tail skid had a rubber string absorber attached to the triangular stabilizing fin. Control surfaces were made of welded steel tubes, covered with canvas skin. The rudder had an aerodynamic corner balance. The **Albatros** was armed with two synchronized 7.92 mm 08/15 caliber LMG Spandau machine guns incorporating a synchronizing device developed by werkmeister Hedtke, later improved by werkmeister Semmler. It proved efficient, particularly when two machine guns were synchronized. In October 1916 the Idflieg required that the Fokker synchronizer be tested on the Albatros but it was prone to malfunction and cut the rate of fire in half. Consequently, Albatros Werke decided against it.

In May 1916 Oblt Rudolf Berthold examined the Albatros D.I serial D.423/16. According to the first edition of his biography, he is believed to have said: *"I am keen on taking the Albatros into combat, we should have a larger force of these excellent aircraft."* He said that to von Thüne from Idejflieg, who allegedly replied: *"I decide which plane goes into battle, not Oblt Berthold."*

Between June 9 and July 7 static trials were successfully conducted. The wing depth was redesigned to be equal, which would also make production easier; aerodynamic corner balance was added to the elevator.

Lt. Von Budde of Jasta 29 in his Albatros D.III 2052/16.

On July 11 Ideflieg recommended Albatos D.I to go into serial production and placed an order for 50 examples (serials D.421-470/16). The evaluation report also included some of the demonstrated performance specs: "it climbs to 5000 m in 38 minutes and achieves 170 km/h in level flight." The first Albatros D.Is were manufactured with the 111 kW (150 hp) Benz Bz III, but with the arrival of the Mercedes engine subsequent machines were fitted with the new powerplant. It made the Albatros heavier but increased the fighter's speed in level flight and in climbs.

The Albatros D.I had excellent aerodynamic qualities for a fighter. Vzfw Carl Holler of Jasta 6 described the new type: *"It has an excellent climb-rate, reaching 5000 m is child's play. It has an excellent dive speed which is important when attacking an enemy below. We no longer have to wait for kills, my two colleagues scored two in a short time."* Unfortunately the author of that statement was shot down by a Nieuport, because he "had not seen" it. Very limited field of view

A later series example of the Albatros D.III with a Teves und Braun radiator offset to the left.

An Albatros D.III from Marine Feld Jagdstaffel 2 in flight.

from the cockpit, c. 30° up and to the sides, turned out to be a serious shortcoming of the Albatros D.I.

The second drawback became apparent in service as the poor visibility of the target hindered accurate aiming, especially at high speeds.

Thirdly, the Windhoff radiator contributed not only to increased drag (thus reducing the plane's performance) but if punctured or in case of a leak (which occurred quite often) the engine absorbed the cooling liquid and ceased, while the hot liquid scalded pilot's face. On November 10, 1916 the use of Windhoff radiators was banned in frontline units.

A design team swiftly addressed all the raised issues. The new, **Albatros D.II (L.17)** version was produced with the upper wing lowered by 30 cm and the support strut pyramid that had obscured forward

visibility was replaced with a new N-shaped, outer support. The first Albatros D.IIs were produced with lateral radiators, but in subsequent examples they were replaced with a new Teves und Braun radiator fitted in the central upper wing. Minor redesign of the fuselage did not delay delivery of further 100 D.IIs (serials D.472- D.521/16 and D.890 – 939/16) ordered in August 1916. Both Albatros variants, the D.I and D.II, were manufactured in parallel. The next order for 100 planes (serials D.1700 – D.1799/16) was placed in September 1916, but since the Albatros works were not able to fulfill the contract on their own, for the first and only time, license-production was assigned in August 1916 to Luft Verkehrs Gesellschaft mbH (LVG) located in nearby Johanisthal. The seventy five examples (serials D.1024/16 – D.1098/16) built at L.V.G. were designated as LVG D.I, only to be re-designated in February 1917 as Albatros (LVG) D.II. They were easily recognizable by their paint scheme, i.e. the characteristic arrangement of color areas on top wing surfaces and the empennage. A total of fifty Albatros D.Is and 275 D.IIs was built at all factories.

A team of designers headed by engineer Thalen focused from the outset on improving the Albatros design. The D.II was selected as the platform they would work on to meet the challenge posed by new aircraft being pressed into service by the French and British, most notably the Nieuport 17C1. One way to go was to further upgrade the fighter's aerodynamic characteristics by making it even sleeker and by re-designing onboard hardware to further minimize drag. The second task was to reduce the weight of Albatros by implementing the latest technologies of wood treatment and, finally, by utilizing enemy's

Albatros D.III 2049/16 flown by Ltn Herman Göring, Jasta 26, April 1917.

An Albatros D.III just before landing.

Lt. Reinhold Oertelt of Jasta 19 and his Albatros D.III 1997/16. The aircraft was from the first production batch. The brace on the cockpit holds a flare pistol. Below there is a container for flare cartridges.

technical solutions, i.e. sesquiplane airframe layout which in fact meant copying the Nieuport design. Not much could be done to re-engine the airframe: the only available powerplants were the Mercedes D.III and Mercedes D.IIIa (a D.III derivative with higher compression ratio and increased capacity) delivering 120-129 kW (170-175 hp) and there were no signs that new, improved and more powerful engines were to arrive soon.

Three designers, Thelen, Schubert and Gnadig built a new version incorporating only minor modifications. Having slightly redesigned the fuselage they applied a new wing arrangement. The upper wing had a 1.50 m chord and a trapezoid shape. The lower wing was of similar shape but its chord was reduced to 1.1. m. Consequently, the team produced a sesquiplane arrangement that replicated the same mistake that had been made by Nieuport designers – the lower wing had only one spar, which reduced its rigidity. Both wings were connected via V-shaped struts. The plane was more maneuverable than its D.I and D.II predecessors and was only a bit inferior to the Nieuport. Powered by the Mercedes D.IIIa engine it had a good speed in level flight and a decent climb-rate. The Albatros D.III 388/16 underwent tests in September 1916 in parallel with the Albatros D.I and D.II. They were successful enough to make Idoflieg immediately order 400 examples (the highest number ever ordered at one time).

Along with the order, a suggestion was filed to use strips as fuselage skin due to shortage of plywood. Five planes were ordered for testing. The outcome was negative as strip-skinned fuselage offered less strength and its weight did not reduce much in com-

A front view of the Albatros' teeth – the twin LMG 08/15 machine guns.

The O.A.W.-built Albatroses from Jasta 50 carried personal insigna painted on fuselages in black and white, and Jasta markings-tailplanes chevron striped blue and red.

parison to plywood-covered counterparts. Consequently, the idea was abandoned, though Roland works took it up and applied in its designs.

In February and March 1917 two more contracts were awarded for 50 planes each. During the production of Albatros D.IIIs a couple of essential refinements were introduced (from serial 2200/16 onwards): the radiator was shifted 0.4 m off the centerline, which improved forward visibility and protected the pilot from exposure to hot engine coolant – a notorious feature of centrally-mounted radiators. Another improvement was strengthened undercarriage.

Albatros D.IIs and D.IIIs manufactured for units operating in Palestine were fitted with twin radiators to improve cooling that even in Europe had been

insufficient enough (the radiators often overheated). Since the Albatros works in Berlin was one of the largest suppliers of aircraft for reconnaissance elements, they could not handle the production of ordered volumes. Production of the Albatros D.III was transferred to the Ostdeutsche Albatros Werke branch in Schneidemühl (present-day Pila). The aircraft manufactured there had the OAW abbreviation added to their designation.

On January 24, 1917 an excellent German pilot Manfred von Richtchoffen engaged a British FE-2B. During the fight he noticed vibrations and a crack in the lower wing. On that same day two other German pilots were killed because the lower wings had torn apart from their Albatros D.IIIs in a dogfight[5]. That was the fault shared with the French Nieuports. It

An Albatros D.III from Jasta 10 . The unit was recognized by its yellow-nosed aircraft.

An L.35 airship in flight with an Albatros D.III (OAW) 3066/17 stowed underneath.

was true, however, for Johanistahl aircraft, whereas it appeared relatively rarely (or never, according to British sources) in D.IIIs manufactured by OAW.

The Albatros D.III also served as a test platform for the Siemens-Kändler machine gun firing through the engine crankshaft and Nebelwerter unguided rocket launchers designed by Lt. R. Nebel to engage enemy's observation balloons.

On January 18, 1918 Albatros D.III(OAW) 3066/17 became the first aircraft ever to launch from Zeppelin L-35 airship. The concept behind an airship-borne fighter was to protect the airship against enemy planes. Though successful, the idea was abandoned only to be revived in the 1930s in the U.S.

In March 1917 Ideflieg ordered a lighter version of the Albatros D.III. A team of designers developed a new plane with much more streamlined fuselage. It had elliptic cross-section and a fairing behind pilot's head. The stabilizing fin was enlarged and a new round-shaped rudder was used. The plane was powered by an experimental Mercedes engine fitted with reduction gear producing 118 kW (160 hp). It was completely embedded in the fuselage and covered with metal cowling. Identical chord wings were restored and linked by single struts. The empennage outline and tailplane surface were changed. Three examples were ordered but only one – designated **Albatros D.IV** – was produced. Unarmed, in September 1917 it underwent Ideflieg trials that revealed strong engine vibrations when using a twin-blade propeller. Though a three- and four-blade propeller was later tested the vibrations did not completely cease and, as a result, in April 1918 further trials were halted to prevent airframe damage. The Mercedes engine equipped with reduction gear turned out to be inadequate for the type.

The **Albatros D.V (L.24)** inherited the fuselage built for Albatros D.IV with its elliptic cross-section stretching throughout the entire fuselage. Behind pilot's head a fairing was fitted, the stabilizing fin underneath the fuselage was enlarged and an oval-shaped rudder developed. Wing design was taken from the Albatros D.III and modified with a new aileron control system (control cables were embedded in the upper wing). A new mount for the lower wing was used. The upper wing was mounted 0.11 m lower than it had been in the Albatros D.III. The plane was also 50 kg lighter than the D.III, but its performance was not much better. Since the modifi-

Lt. Rudolf Hohberg's Albatros D.III 1996/16 of Flieger Abteilung(A) 263 adapted to reconnaissance missions. The fuselage is painted in light blue and dark green, upper surfaces of wings and tailplane in three color Terrain Camouflage.

The Heinecke parachute seen here fitted to the fuselage of a D.III was pilot's last resort. On the side are flare gun rounds.

cations were not considered major, endurance tests were skipped and in June 1917 the design entered serial production at the Johannistahl plant. Three orders for the total of 900 aircraft (serials D1000 – D1199/17; D1962 – D2361/17; D4403 – 4702/17 respectively) were placed.

The first Albatros D.Vs reached combat units in June 1917 and instead of expected major victories there was a series of disasters. The new, weaker, ferrule that coupled the lower wing with the fuselage and poor wing mount changed the center of pressure-spar[6] axis arrangement, leading to the lower wings tearing away, mostly when recovering from a dive. The Albatros D.III also suffered from that, but not that often. Introduction of a support connecting the leading edge with the strut turned out to be a simple and relatively effective way of strengthening the structure, hence limiting but not eliminating the possibility of twisting the narrow lower wing. Besides the Albatros D.V, the D.III produced in parallel was soon also fitted with the support. However there was still no clear understanding of what design shortcomings had contributed to the lower wing failures.

A German top-scoring ace Ernst Udet described in his memoirs how he had been trying to avoid the worst. "When I was beginning a steep dive I looked at the lower wing and when I noticed it had started to flatter I knew it was time to recover or I would lose my wings."

According to unofficial records, the German air service lost more Albatros fighters to accidents than to enemy action. But tearing away of the wings did not immediately mean a plane crash since a lot still depended on pilot's skills. For instance, though Lt. Joachim von Hippel flying a D.V of Jasta 6 lost both wings in fight he still managed to land because the ailerons control cables in the upper wing and the fuselage were fully serviceable.

Another deficiency of the plane was the fairing behind pilot's head since it obscured visibility to the aft. For that reason it was removed at repair workshops and with time also the factories stopped fitting them in serial production. Furthermore, the aileron control system that had proven itself on the D.III (control cables ran through the lower wing to a lever with aileron upper wing). An aileron lock system (stick lock) was added to allow the pilot to unjam machine guns with both hands.

With such modifications the plane was designated **Albatros D.Va** and entered serial production in October 1917. The Albatros became the most numerous type in fighter units.

The Albatros D.Va was manufactured under separate orders with the following serials: D5165-D5426/17, D5600-5849/17 and D7000-D7549/17 respectively, with the Ostdeutsce Albatros Werke at Schneidemuhl D.Va(OAW)s numbered D6400-6999/17 (1662 examples altogether).

Noteworthy are the attempts to upgrade the Albatros firepower. Copying the Entente solution, an Albatros D.V was fitted with a captured Lewis machine gun mounted on a specially designed cradle. Another attempt was also undertaken to install twin Villar Perosa machine guns on the upper wing. However, the increased firepower did not make up for the increased weight and downgraded performance. The concept of the second machine gun on the upper wing did not last long in the German air arm. In November 1916 a single Albatros D.II was armed with a Becker cannon and sent for testing to Ideflieg from where it proceeded for further evaluation in a frontline unit.

Attempts were also made to boost firepower. In February 1918, two Siemens-Schuckert machine guns firing 1400 rpm. were fitted onto two Albatros D.Vas, which were sent to Jasta 5. Responsibility over installation of the armament was given to engineer Kändler. The fighters were flown by Vfws. Josef Mai and Fritz Rumey. The latter shot down a DH4 on Feb. 26 scoring his 9th kill. The new armament arrangement was not cleared as it was too troublesome. The two Albatroses featured white bones with black rims under the cockpit edge. Rumey's plane also sported black diagonal stripes on the fuselage.

A number of D.IIIs and D.Vas were equipped with dedicated camera grips (on the starboard side of the cockpit). Such planes were used for reconnaissance[7] by the Flieger Abteilung 259 among others.

An Albatros D.V[8], serial 7117/17 was fitted with a 137 kW (185 hp) BMW IIIa engine. On February 6, 1918 the plane broke the altitude record by climbing to 10500 m, although the achievement could not be officially acknowledged as the onboard barometer had not been properly certified. Planned deliveries of the B.M.W. engines for Albatros D.Va had to succumb to changing military requirements as the new Fokker D.VII[9] received top priority for production and all BMW shipments were diverted to the Fokker plant.

The Albatros works followed the WW1 trend of building triplanes and decided to build the **Albatros Dr.I (L.36)** – a fighter triplane based on the Albatros D.Va design. Its fuselage was fitted with three identical wings: the upper and lower wings had unified structures and were mounted to the fuselage using struts, while the middle wing was split and coupled with the fuselage. The wing featured cutouts to improve the field of view beneath the plane. All three wings were connected with twin struts and had ailerons[10] linked together by single steel struts. Aileron controls went through the middle wing. The engine was cooled with modified twin Teves und Braun radiators installed on the upper wing. The aircraft began the test program at Ideflieg in 1917, but it was not completed as the modified radiators offered insufficient cooling.

In September 1917, a prototype of **Albatros D.VII** fighter was built. It was powered by the 144 kW (195 hp), V-8 Benz Bz IIIb engine. Both wings were of

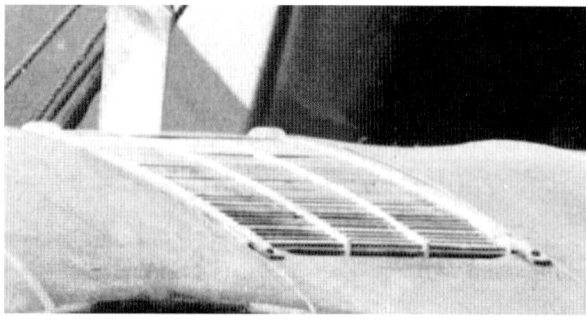

Teeves und Braun radiator

Daimler Mercedes radiator

identical span and depth, and had ailerons . The empennage outline was changed to a shape resembling that of the Albatros C.XV. The plane had a quite good level speed and climb-rate. It had faced, however, interrupted engine deliveries and met with no interest from Ideflieg, which eventually led to cancellation of further development.

For the second fighter competition the Albatros works came up with a number of prototype fighters, among them the **Albatros D.IX**, **Albatros D.X** and **Albatros D.XII** (serial D 2210/18) with inline engines, and the Albatros D.XI (D 2295/18 and D2209/18) powered by the 118 kW Siemens-Halske Sh.III ro-

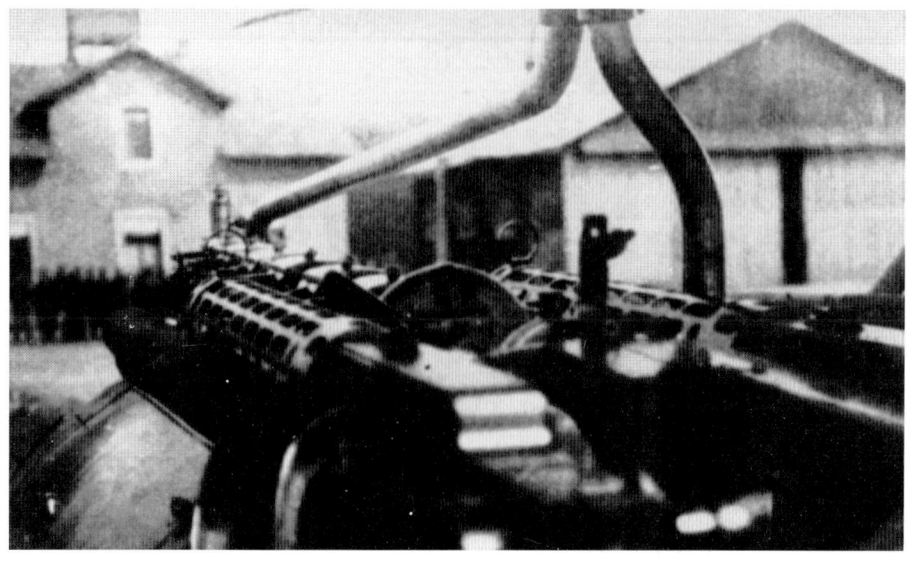

View from an Albatros D.V's cockpit.

The Albatros D.IV prototype was fitted with a closely-cowled specially-geared Mercedes engine.

A prototype of the Albatros D.V completely covered in five-color lozenge camouflage. The rudder was taken from Albatros D.III.

tary engine. Despite its good level speed (190 km/h), climb rate of 15000 m in 15'1 min., and maneuverability it was not cleared for serial production. The inline engine prototypes did not go into regular production either. In the third fighter competition the second Albatros D.XII prototype with the 137 kW BMW IIIa engine was fielded, but was not selected for serial production.

In 1918 another triplane was built – the **Albatros Dr.II**. Its design was based on the D.X, but simplified in comparison with the Dr.I that had featured wings similar to those of the Sopwith Triplane. Though the Albatros was powered by the Benz IVb engine pro-

ducing 145 kW, it offered poor performance as the frontally-mounted radiator between the upper and middle wing increased drag. Further development was cancelled.

In 1918 Naglo Bootswerft from the Spandau works designed a quad-plane based on the Albatros D.V fuselage, but it did not go past the prototype test stage.

Naval Aviation

The German Navy HQ was interested in a fighter floatplanes and at the turn of May and June 1916, it invited Albatros, Friedrichshafen, Hansa-Brandenburg, Lubeck-Travemunde, Roland, Rumpler and Sablating to build one. On May 16 an order was placed for three fighter floatplanes at an Albatros branch in Friedrichshafen on the Müggelsee (the largest lake near Berlin). Designated serial numbers 747, 785 and 786, the type was powered by a liquid-cooled inline engine delivering 118 kW (160 hp). Its armament consisted of a single machine gun. Relatively shortly, on August 28, 1916, the Seeflugzeug Versuchs Kommando (SVK) naval research and test center at Warnemünde received the first **Albatros W. 4** (Wasserflugzeuge), serial **747**. Its design was based on the Albatros D.I. The plane was followed by its competitors, Rumpler 6B1 (serial 751) and Friedrichshafen FF44 (serial 749) delivered to SVK for tests.

The Albatros W.4 design did not differ much from the D.II. The tailplane was given a new outline and top strut support, the far stabilizing fin was removed and instead of the regular undercarriage two floats were fitted. They turned to be too short and subsequent prototypes, serials 747 and 785 from the outset had new, elongated floats. All in all, the Albatros was

An Albatros W 4 prototype with marine number 747. The aircraft is in „plain" finish.

An OAW-manufactured Albatros D.V.

a much better design than its competitors and on September 5, 1916 an order was placed for a test batch comprising serials 902-911. The order had been completed by February 1917. The third prototype (786) received all the upgrades that had been suggested by test pilots evaluating the first two prototypes and delivered to SVK in December 1916. The floats suffered from further teething problems, the biggest of which was poor structural strength. Upon contact with sea water their fatigue progressed so rapidly that inspections were ordered after each sortie. A similar problem existed with the lower wing, which due to humidity suffered from structural (spar) failures. Production of fully waterproof wings was ordered. The floats were strengthened and better impregnation applied. Throughout the service life the shape of floats was redesigned a number of times to improve

their seaworthiness. The arrangement of struts and legs was changed, and transparent celluloid skin of the wing central section was replaced with canvas. In June 1917 planes from the fifth production run (serials 1484-1513) onwards were fitted with new Teves und Braun radiators as the previously used Windhoff radiators were prone to overheating on warm days. Firepower was also increased by adopting a twin gun arrangement implemented in an aircraft batch starting with serials 945-967.

The Albatros W.4 was built in seven[11] production runs totaling 106 examples (Navy serials 945-967, 1107-1116, 1302-1326, 1484-1503 and 1719-1738).

In terms of maneuverability, level speed, climb-rate and field of view, the Albatros W.4 was far better than the Hansa Brandenburg KDW the Navy had been flying. Its superiority was proven in a mock

An Albatros W. 4 (marine serial 1512) with ailerons on both wings. The aircraft is finished in full camouflage with naval hexagons painted on all upper surfaces, side surfaces and struts in grey blue, fuselage undersurfaces in light grey, under wing and tailplane surfaces clear – dopped fabric.

An Albatros D.V armed with Italian Villar Perosa machine guns.

Albatros D.V fitted with a captured Lewis machine gun.

dogfight between pilots trained at the Jasta Schule in Valanciennes against their KDW colleagues.

In June 1917 serials 1312 underwent a series of modifications: aileron surfaces and the lower wing were enlarged, but these attempts to enhance maneuverability backfired by downgrading flight performance. That same month, float legs were shortened on serial 1318. In July 1917 serial 1484, featuring ailerons on the upper and lower wings connected with a strut, made its maiden flight. The upper wing ailerons were shortened by one rib. The modified plane was more maneuverable, but performed worse. Endurance tests of the new design were successfully conducted on the 1495. One of the W.4s was also a test platform for an electric synchronizer.

Most (91) of the ordered Albatros W.4s were delivered between June and December 1917. They were rated Klasse I and cleared to serve in any conditions. Twenty four planes were assigned to training duties at a number of naval air bases/stations, including one in Puck (Putzig) on the Baltic coast.

Survivability – seaworthiness – of the Albatros W.4 was proven when the serial 960 flown by Flugobermat Pönig ditched in the rough waters of the North Sea after he had suffered an engine malfunction. Upon ditching he slipped out of the cockpit towards the empennage trying to balance the plane upwards and prevent it from being flooded by the swells. He managed to do so for 6 hours until the wind and waves subsided. Only then did he climb on the upper wing. After a few hours he was picked up by a torpedo boat that had been sent out to search for the missing plane.

An Albatros Dr.II.

Lt. Ernst Bauer of Flieger Abteilung 259 in the cockpit of his Albatros D.V. Bauer's Albatros was fitted with a camera mount.

Further orders for Albatros W.4 were cancelled in favor of rival Brandenburg W 12 and Friedrichshafen FF 33 fighters. They offered better armament, higher payloads and superior endurance, while two crewmembers ensured safer missions. Following the shift to the new aircraft, the last W.4s, serials 1719-1739, were handed over directly to a military depot in Hage. When the war ended, the Allied Cease-fire Committee recorded in December 1918 67 Albatros W.4s.

In exchange for a shipment of Austro-Daimler V-12 engines for Staaken bombers, 8 W.4s (serials 1317, 1318, 1326, 1504, 1505, 1506, 1507 and 1608) were given to Austro-Hungary. They had been originally acquired for the naval aviation service – the **K.u.K. Seeflugwesen** – but in July 1918 they reached the new user. They were re-designated E5 to E12 and assigned to Trieste. No information is available on their combat record.

Better Than the Original

When Austro-Hungary declared war on Serbia on July 28, 1914, they did not have much of a an air force. An aviation unit – the Kaiserische und Königlishe Luftfahrtruppen[12] (k.u.k. LFT for short) had officially existed since 1912 and in reality since 1893, when the Balloon Corps was formed. Austro-Hungary entered the war with 39 aircraft, 10 balloons and 85 trained pilots. Plane production was the domain of Jakob Lohner & CO., Warchalowski, Eissler & CO (Hiero), Ernst böhm. Mähr. Maschinen Fabrik (Prague) and Werner&Pflelderer. Engines were manufactured by Austro-Daimler at Wiener-Neustadt. Neither indigenous plants nor hardware imported from German factories originally coped with the overwhelming requirement for new equipment. On March 3, 1915,

Oesterreichische Flugzeugfabrik A.G. (Oeffag) was established in Wiener-Steinnfield on the outskirts of Steinnfield, where production of aircraft, including the Albatros D.II (Oef) and D.III (Oef) was set up.

The k.u.k LFT HQ closely monitored fighter competitions in Germany, where experienced Austrian pilots[13] were sent to gather information useful in the process of procuring planes or a license for production in Austria. Such was the case with the Albatros fighters – in the fall of 1916 a manufacturing license for Albatros D.II was secured and its production implemented[14] at Österreichische Flugzeugfabrik AG. A prototype of the **Albatros D.II(Oef)**[15] marked 53.01[16] was first flown in January 1917. It was not an exact copy of the German Albatros D.II as it had a different powerplant – the Austro-Daimler Dm 185 producing 136 kW (185 KM). Cylinders that in

A unique photo showing a dogfight between an Albators and a British S.E.5a.

Rittm Manfred von Richtchofen's battle-damaged Albatros D.Va. On Jul. 6, during a dogfight with an FE 2B from No. 20 Sqn the Red Baron suffered a nearly fatal head wound.

the original stuck out from the fuselage were completely covered by aluminum cowling. Wing surfaces were enlarged by increasing their chords by 10 cm in comparison to the German design (170 cm). Consequently, the lifting surfaces were enlarged which compensated for the increased engine weight (the Austro-Daimler was heavier than the Mercedes) and ensured wing load similar to the German original.

Moreover, liquid coolers were fitted on the upper wing just like in the late German examples.

Unlike the original armed with two machine guns, Albatros D.II(Oef) had only one – 8 mm Schwarzlose M 7/12 – fitted in the fuselage (in the original the gun was mounted externally), right off the centerline. Shots fired went below engine exhaust pipes through a tube from the barrel to a port in the front part of

Kpr. Pil. Antoni Bartkowiak standing next to his Albatros D.V 7177/17 in which he escaped from Bydgoszcz(Bromberg) to Poznań. The plane served with the 2nd „Wielkopolska" Aviation Squadron.

the engine. The arrangement prevented the ignition of discharge gases concentrated in the front part of the fuselage from igniting. Moreover, with such positioning of the machine gun, the ammunition belt would be heated to prevent it from stiffening at low temperatures and jamming. This produced aerodynamic benefits, but on the other hand it made it impossible to re-cock a gun or unjam it in flight.

Apart from better aerodynamic features, visibility from the cockpit was also improved.

Positioning the armament in the front part of the fuselage made it necessary to introduce an additional fuel tank inside the upper wing, left of the centerline.

On December 4, 1916, the LFT officially ordered 50 Albatros D.II (Oef)s, but after completion of the 15th example (serials 53.02-53.16) production was halted. The reason for this was the new Albatros D.III version that had been developed at the turn of September and October 1916. Austria immediately secured a license for the plane and the Oeffag works were ordered to resume production, but of the latest D.III variant. However, since all the fuselages had already been produced at the Wiener-Neustadt in keeping with the original specs, only the wings and their wing bays were manufactured according to the new documentation.

In February 1917, the **Albatros D.III (Oef)** prototype, marked 53.20, was built and flown. Though the overall geometry of the original design was kept, the plane differed in that it had cylinder cowling and a triangular part was added under the fuselage to enlarge the stabilizing fin. Its armament consisted of twin Scharzlose m07/12 machine guns that were fitted inside the fuselage, similarly to the D.II (Oef) var-

iant. However, the first examples, e.g. 53.22, rolled-out with only one gun – on the starboard side. The type also featured the rigging angle adjustment for the upper wing, gravity-fed a fuel tank inside and an airfoil Hirschfelder radiator was placed on the wing symmetry axle. The position of the radiator remained unchanged despite the fact it had been moved[17] off to the right in the German models. What was characteristic of the Austrian Albatros D.III (Oef) was that its engine was completely[18] enclosed by a cowling made of metal sheets and simple, horizontal exhaust pipes from each of the 6 cylinders. Some examples of the D.II (Oef) and D.III (Oef) had collective exhaust systems, e.g. serials 53.22, 53.28, 53.29 and the prototype 153.01. After completion of the airworthiness tests in early May 1917, a recommendation was issued to strengthen[19] the lower wing coupling according to a solution developed by technicians at Wiener-Neustadt.

Strength of the lower wing increased: wooden spar stripes were thickened by 10 mm, ribs were made of thicker plywood, the way ribs were coupled with the spar was changed and a metal block with 'Z' cross-section was introduced to strengthen the mount of the front auxiliary spar under the fuselage – thus virtually killing the flatter effect. In spite of that, some D.III (Oef)s like their German counterparts, received an extra support bracket from the front strut to the wing's leading edge. That improvement was installed e.g. on D.III (Oef) 53.37, 53.39. Serial production was launched on May 26, 1917. By the end of June 1917, 45 examples of the new type were built and joined Fliegerkompagnien[20] (Flik) 19, 32, 33, 35, 40, 42, 46, 47 and 48.

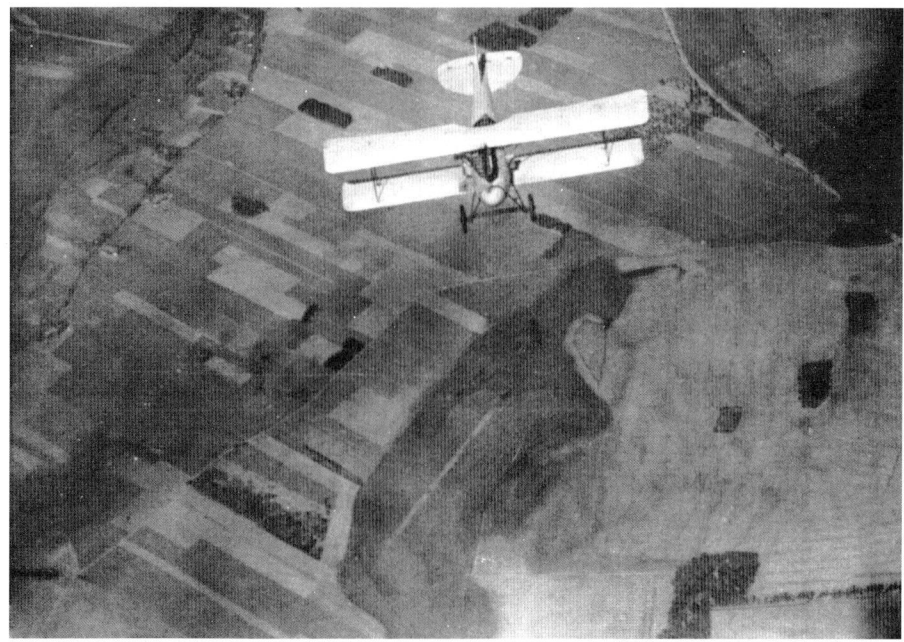

A Polish Albatros D.II seen in flight over Wielkopolska.

Palenie tytoniu wzbronione

The Albatros D.II (Oef) and D.III (Oef) had good longitudinal and lateral stability, they were maneuverable and easy to fly. They were also slightly faster (20-25 km/h) and had higher climb-rates than their German counterparts. Manufactured with greater attention, their survivability was also greater. As far as maneuverability and climb-rate was concerned, they were superior to combat Hansa-Brandenburgs, yet their level speed was comparable. An additional merit of the D.III was that it was easy to fly. One report on the type stated: "A pilot without prior training could fly the Albatros." The fact was indirectly confirmed by

Capt. Meriam Cooper in his book when he described his first contact with the Albatros D.III in Lwów.

"We could see four or five airplanes on the training ground, each a single-seater. These were the Albatros D-3 airplanes we were to receive and fly in service.

Having greeted us the Polish officers took off and delivered an excellent show of their piloting skills. We were exquisitely pleased with the company of pilots we got to serve with. Most of us had not been flying at least for a year, so we doubted we could be on a par with them. We were afraid that once we took

The Ławica assembly line – in the foreground an Albatros D.III.

Eventually he side-slipped the aircraft and landed successfully. We enjoyed his show immensely, but Faunt-le-Roy berated him for recklessly taking risks on a new plane he had not been proficient on.

The Oeffag-built Albatros fuselages allowed the use of more powerful though heavier engines without major modifications of the design – such was the concept followed by Oeffag's designers. In the spring of 1917 Ferdinand Porsche developed a 147-kW (200 hp) Austro-Daimler engine introduced on subsequent D.III (Oef) examples. The new planes, featuring also the upper wing moved forward by c. 2 cm (in respect to Albatros D.III (Oef) series 53) in order to retain the center of gravity, were marked **Bauart 153** (Ba.153 for short). The LFK ordered 280 of those. Production commenced in July 1917, and soon a problem occurred with selecting a suitable propeller for the new engine. Several propellers were tested on serial 153.01 until the most optimal was found. Serial production started in July 1917. Like the series 53 model, the new type had the engine covered with cowling and was deprived of the exhaust manifold.

In field operations environment the propeller spinner often tore away in-flight, imminently creating the risk of structural damage, so the pilots removed it and flew without it. This also improved oil cooling as the oil tank was in the front part of the fuselage, right behind the spinner. A number of planes rolled out of the factory without spinners. The design team addressed the issue and developed a new streamlined nose section of the fuselage. Among other minor modifications was the relocation of the fuel feed lines closer to the rear of the fuselage. The 153 series with redesigned front fuselage section was 9 km/h faster in level flight than the spinner-equipped planes. It also had a slightly higher climb-rate. Examples with new front sections received serial numbers 112 through 281. In some late 153 series examples ailerons and tailplane trailing edges were fitted with wires replacing steel tubes. Wing and rudder trailing edges had characteristic concavities.

Hpt. Brumowski proved how tough series 153 Albatros D.III (Oef) really were when flying a 153.45. On February 1, 1918, his upper wing gravity tank was hit during a dogfight. The fuel ignited and flames started to chew the skin. The pilot entered a steep dive and increased airflow put out the fire. Despite losing about 40% of skin on the right upper and lower wing, he managed to nurse the plane home and land successfully.

Another deficiency of the Albatros D.III (Oef) troubling the pilots were the machine guns embed-

off we would crash a few planes on our first 'go' but thanks to instructions and leadership of Col. Faunt-le-Roy we held our own quite well.

Faunt-le-Roy flew perfectly though I knew he had not been at the controls for at least ten months. When he landed Lt. Graves went up. The memory of his flight is still fresh . He accelerated like crazy still on the ground, started a U-turn constantly tightening the radius of his circle while his lower wing was almost skidding on the ground. After completing a full circle he got airborne and delivered the most difficult, yet the best show of pilot skills I had ever seen.

Albatros D.IIIs and D.Vs repaired at Ławica. The photo was taken in March 1919.

ded in the fuselage and synchronizers[21] that often malfunctioned. As the guns often jammed, makeshift modifications were introduced by combat units. For instance, twin Schwarzlose M7/12 machine guns were mounted underneath the central section of the upper wing to shoot outside the propeller arc. Such changes were made on Hauptman (Capt.) Godwin Brumowski's Albatros D.III (Oef) 53.30 from Flik 41J. Offiziersstellvertreter Kurt Gruber flying the Albatros D.III (Oef) 153.12 troubleshot the problem differently – to the left of cockpit he put an additional machine gun firing outside the propeller. Another pilot, Julius Arigi flying the D. III (Oef) 53.20 increased firepower by fitting the third, unsynchronized Schwarzlose M7/12 machine gun on the upper wing. Those solutions were not popular among the airmen and not copied on any other plane.

Problems with the armament made the designers address the issue and copy the concept applied on the German original – to remove the machine guns from inside and put them on the fuselage. The modification was implemented on Albatros D.III (Oef) serials 153.161, 153.162 and 153.181 that were handed over to Flik 61/J for evaluation and feedback. The machine guns were placed so that the rounds went over exhaust pipes, away from carburetors. Spent casings were ejected outside using a tube on the left, in front of the cockpit. Ammunition belts were fed through a convex shell reducing drag. Backs of the guns were covered with soft pads protecting the pilots against injuries in case of a hard or crash-landing. Armament tests were conducted using the serial 153.109 at Waffenversuchsflik[22] in Fischamend, with particular focus on synchronizers to select their best setup.

The Albatros D.III(Oef) 153 series was further subject to modifications. Attempts were made to fit them with cameras and radio transceivers. The plant manufactured 9 153-series examples in the photo-recce variant but they had worse performance due to underpowered engines. The recce Albatros D.III (Oef)s were assigned to reconnaissance Flik 12/Rb, 36/K, 37/P, 40/P (the example 153.113)[23] and 48/P.

Pilots flying them were not very successful. The attempts to fit serials 153.32 and 153.135 with radios were equally ill-fated. Electronic equipment was at that time far from perfect, large and heavy. Moreover, to operate it the pilot had to have additional skills, including familiarization with the Morse code, not to mention that operating the radio was so absorbing that the pilot could forget about the flying the plane.

Stabsfeldwebel (staff sergeant) Friedrich Hefty from Flik 42, 7 kills, best expressed an opinion that the 153 series Albatros D.III (Oef) enjoyed: "with the 200-hp engine this is an excellent airplane, perfectly balanced, ideal for acrobatics. Its climb-rate is equal to Hanriot and Camel, though it lags behind the Spad in level flight."

Plt. Lt. Jach and an Albatros D.III. The white-painted aircraft may have belonged to ZAK-3.

Plt. Lt. Jach in the cockpit of the D.III which he flew during a successful mission against a Soviet observation balloon.

Between July 1917 and June 1918, 281 series 153 aircraft were built[24] (serials 153.01 through 153.281). Pilots who flew the type liked it and 25 of them scored three or more victories. In August 1918, 142 examples of series 153 Albatros D.III (Oef) were in service with combat units, most surviving until the cease of hostilities.

The series 3 (Bauart 3) was powered by the 166 kW (225 hp) Austro-Daimler engine, but it required that certain design changes in the aircraft be made. Fuselage structure was strengthened with additional diagonal struts applied in its aft section. Wingtips were reinforced with plywood elements. Moreover,

following in the footsteps of series 153 some examples received steel wire for aileron and the elevator trailing edges. Modifications were implemented gradually, but some planes[25] could still be seen with original parts. This might have been due to a shortage of materials on stock at the production plant or ad hoc overhauls performed in the field by military personnel who utilized available[26] parts from other series aircraft.

The first order for 230 series 3 D.III (Oef)s was placed on May 18, 1918 and soon it was extended to further 100 planes (assigned serials 253.231-253.330). Production pace was fast and the first 9 series 253 fighters reached Fliks[27] 61 and 63 late the same month.

As was the case with the three series 153 examples, also series 253 saw a number of Albatros D.III (Oef)s (serials 253.31, 253.64, 253.116-120 among them) fitted with machine guns closer to the fuselage crest. Their barrels were underneath cowling over exhaust pipes (easily identified on existing pictures). Like previous Albatros series, most of the 253-series D.IIIs had engines completely embedded with individual exhaust pipes per each cylinder.

Moreover, like in the series 153 a single 253-series example also underwent trials with 50 cm focal length camera. Later it was assigned to Flik 40/P.

Pilots had generally good opinion of the Albatros. When asked by LFT personnel what type of aircraft they would order, the reply was: "It is the best, fastest, most robust and maneuverable fighter in the line." Such a statement might have been an exaggeration but in comparison to other types used by the Austro-Hungarian air service it was pretty true[28]. The 253 series Albatros was on par with Italian and British fighters particularly on the Italian Front.

Adam Haber Włyński's Albatros D.III.

An Albatros D.III belonging to the Warsaw-based Aviation Observer School. Spring 1919.

A collision between an Albatros D.III 1835 and a Rumpler C.I .

An Albatros D.VII.

An Albatros D.IX.

An Albatros D.XI (D 2209/18).

The praise was substantiated during a *Bewertungsfliegen* evaluation held on July 9-13, 1918 at Vienna-Aspern. Similar to German competitions, 26 aircraft ran in the D-Flugzeug Wettbewerb fighter event, including two series 253 Albatros D.III (Oef) s, serials 253.32 and 253. 35. They had almost the best climb-rates, giving way only to prototype WKF 80.10 and series 338.03 Aviatik-Berg D.I. Further trials were conducted only with D.III (Oef) 253.64 and Berg D.I 338.06. The former got the most positive marks and the Oeffag plant got priority in receiving the 166 kW (225 hp) Austro-Daimler engines, thus priority was given to production of Albatros D.III (Oef) series 253.

Finally, evidence must be given to a multi-pronged path Albatros (Oef)s followed from the plant to a combat unit. First a plane was checked by a *Bauafsicht* military inspector residing at every plant. After he cleared an example, it was sent to one of *Fliegerarsenal*, FLARS[29] for short, where the plane underwent further tests From there it went to one of eleven *Fliegeretappenpark*, or FLEPS[30]. This was the last place before a fighter reached a Flik combat unit. On rare occasions the Fleps stop was skipped.

By the end of hostilities 201 examples had been delivered. Production was continued after the war until 260 series 253[31] aircraft had been produced.

Albatros D.III Design

The Albatros D.III was a wooden, single-engine, single seat, sesquiplane fighter.

The fuselage - semi-monocoque had a longitudinal frame structure covered with plywood skin. Its cross section varied depending on airframe sections: it was round at the nose, elliptical at the engine compartment, round at the top and flat at the bottom with flat sides up to the heavily flattened tail section.

An Albatros Dr.II.

The plywood skin was 2 mm thick and was shaped hot under pressure. Then it was glued to frames and four ash longerons, nailed or screwed down using brass screws. Each sheet was attached to the other at the frames and longerons. However, the Kraków-based facility used plywood stripes to simplify the production and repairs made on the Albatros D.III (Oef).

Frames at the bottom of the engine compartment were much thicker than any other on the aircraft and to reduce their weight dedicated holes were bored in them. Onto those frames wooden beams were mounted that served as an engine cradle. Moving aft, there was a frame that separated the engine compartment from the cockpit with a thin plywood bulkhead. Underneath the cockpit floor special plywood semi-frames were fitted to strengthen the fuselage throughout the cockpit section. The engine compartment was covered with detachable aluminum sheets that were coupled using snap fasteners. Peepholes and ventilation ports had special-shaped aluminum sheet cowling. At the lower wing root the fuselage was flat and protruded outboard. The protrusion front and end received dedicated extruded aluminum sheet cowling that was nailed to the skin. The tail section sported two tubes that were used for

The second Albatros D.XII prototype (D.2211/18).

assembling the tailplane with a threaded rod with a screw cap that prevented the tailplane from sliding away.

Inside the fuselage, in front of the cockpit there was a special yoke designed for the fighter's two machine guns. It was made from welded steel tubes and dedicated formers.

The control surfaces - wooden elliptic-shaped **tailplane** comprised of a single-spar, plywood-skinned vertical fin that was integral to the fuselage and a two-spar, sectional, canvas covered horizontal stabilizer. The trailing edge of latter was in line with the tail fuselage edge. Four metal hinges coupled its control surfaces. The surfaces made of steel tubes covered with canvas were also fitted with corner aerodynamic balance.

The rudder was attached to the vertical fin by two hinges with its leading edge extending over the fuselage centerline. In line with the yaw axis a special lever was installed and linked with cables to a rudder bar.

The tailplane control surfaces moved around their front framework tube. It was welded to two levers made of extruded steel sheet which were linked with cables to the control stick.

The Albatros D.III depending on its version and production site appeared with two types of the rudder: straight (the Albatros (Oef) was fitted exclusively with that variation) or round trailing edge (typical for the Albatros D.V manufactured at OAW in Piła). Underneath the tail section of the fuselage a special triangle plywood-covered stabilizing fin was fitted. Like the rudder above it, the fin constituted an integral element of the airframe. Its variation was unveiled with the Albatros (Oef) which featured an enlarged fin with a more oblique trailing edge. In Poland the fighters that underwent repairs at Kraków were refitted with the German-style D.III fins.

The upper wing, one-piece two-spar was attached to the fuselage via four N-shaped steel tube supports. Its framework was composed of two spars, the leading edge, 28 ribs, a support spar and 7 drag struts between the spars with steel strings. The box spar was made of two wooden strips connected using plywood walls. Where ferrule was to fitted dedicated wooden inserts were glued to increase rigidity of the structure. The front spar was located close to the leading edge (at 10% of the chord) while the rear spar at 60% of the chord measured from the leading edge. The spars were linked via thin steel tube drag struts coupled in the ferrule screwed to the spars. These had lugs for steel wire strings. To the right of the wing center section, between the spars there was a rectangular bay to house a liquid cooler. The support spar was in fact a l-bar wooden beam fitted with five hinges to move ailerons. Positions of the aileron

Lt. Ludwig Hanstein from Jasta 37 in the cockpit of Albatros D.V. His Albatros was overpainted in a silver grey finish, with dark green dapple camouflage. Under the cockpit there is a grip for flare pistol rounds.

A two color Terrain Camouflage scheme used on all Albatros D.Is from production batch D.421- 435/16.

drives marked sections of the beam. In the middle of the upper wing there was a special semi-elliptic cutaway to improve visibility upwards.

The ribs were composed of ash strips (so-called shelves) and lime boards constituting their walls (so-called soul). The rib shelves gripped the spars from the top and bottom. To reduce the weight of the design special holes were drilled in the ribs.

A three color Terrain Camouflage scheme used on L.V.G. Build Albatros D.II from batch 1024 – 1098.

The wooden leading edge was located between the second and last but one rib (counted from the left to the right) of the wing. The space between the leading edge and the front spar was covered from above with plywood.

The trailing edge was in fact a steel wire attached to the extremes of ribs, though the Albatros D.III (Oef) was fitted either with a steel tube or the wire.

The upper wing was equipped with eight ferrules made of steel sheets, screw through and through the spar and secured using screw caps. The ferrule was designed to couple the wing with the support structure connecting it with the fuselage, hold the inter-wing struts and to tie strings that strengthen the wing bay. As described elsewhere herein, the D.III (Oef) also received another dedicated wing support element.

The ailerons were located only on the upper wing. Their structure was made of metal tubes welded together and covered with canvas forming a wash-in. In their mid-section there was a two-arm lever with tied aileron drive strings running down to the lower wing. The trailing edge was a steel wire, though the Albatros D.III (Oef) was fitted either with a steel tube or the wire.

The lower wing was split, single-spar, mounted to the fuselage using single-point ferrules. The wing had a smaller span and shorter chord than its upper counterpart, but their aerofoil was similar. The **lower wing** was built around a single box spar located at the third of the chord's length. From the leading edge up to a wooden board running across the whole wing span and fixed to the spar using three spars, had plywood skin. The wing had 12 ribs. The first two inboard ribs were covered with plywood as well, but there was maintenance gap cutout to enable access to the wing-to-fuselage mount ferrule. The thick inboard rib was bored near the ferrule to make space for a bolt keeping the wing in place. Throughout its whole span up to the inter-wing strut ran an aluminum duct leading the aileron control cables. In the wing root area the leading edge was supported against a sheet metal frame that worked as a blocking element keeping the wing fixed in respect to the fighter's centerline. The Albatros D.III (Oef) offered also a dedicated wing support design which has been discussed herein.

The wing bay had only one span. A V-shaped strut connected the lower wing with the upper, with a steel string arrangement to increase its rigidity. The fuselage was fitted with ferrules used for bolting brackets and strings. To eliminate the troubling flattering of the lower wing an auxiliary rigidity improvement was devised that went from the strut with the leading edge. The new element was rarely used on the Albatros D.III (Oef).

Noteworthy is the fact that D.III's wings were interchangeable with the D.Va.

The control system was composed of manually- and leg-operated controls, i.e. the stick and rudder bar. The former was made of a twisted tube and control grip handles revolving around a bolt. The tube was set in a two bearing coupling with a single arm lever holding aileron control cables. The elevator control cables were attached to pins welded on either side of the control stick. The rudder bar was more simple as it was in fact just a steel tube with a bulge in the middle to hold strings running through two blocks up to the rudder.

The undercarriage unit was fitted underneath the fuselage using shoes. It was a twin leg system made of welded steel tubes which had oval-cross sections. A connecting link between the front and rear leg formed a V-shaped element. At the point of connection the rear leg had special ears to hold a joint-mounted, bolted transverse strut strengthening the undercarriage. The ears also had a fixture for intersecting lines that strengthened the rear legs. Their other end was fastened in a set of lanyards located in semicircular cups. The wheel axle consisted of a single element mounted to the legs using a rubber hose. The axle and the strut were embedded in an aerodynamic plywood fairing. The 700x100 wheels had their spokes covered with canvas to reduce drag.

The tail skid was made of ash wood covered with a canvas tape. Its wooden arm was fitted with a metal shoe. The whole element was fastened to the triangle stabilizing fin using a joint. A rubber hose that served as a shock absorber was threaded through a ferruled port in the fin.

The powerplant was a six cylinder, liquid-cooled Mercedes D.III producing 118 kW (160 hp) or alternatively a D.IIIa with improved compression ratio offering 126-129 kW (170-175 hp). Power was transferred to a twin-blade, fixed pitch propeller with the hub covered by an aerodynamic spinner. Propellers from three different manufacturers (Axial, Niendorf and Wolf) were used. The Teeves & Braun radiator fitted with a liquid cooler was located on the

Albatros D.III from Jasta 29 with clearly visible three color camouflage on wings and tail. Note black number "1" on the fuselage sides and top.

upper wing. On some examples (especially in the D.V and D.Va variants) Daimler Mercedes radiators were used.

The fuel tank was located between the engine and the cockpit. It had the capacity of 80 l and was augmented by an additional reserve 22 l tank under the pilot's seat. An 8 l oil tank was fitted under the engine block.

The Austro-Hungarian variant of the Albatros – the D.III (Oef) Ba.253 was powered by a six cylinder, liquid-cooled Austro-Daimler producing 168 kW (225 hp). Its output was transmitted to a wooden twin-blade, fixed pitch propeller. The engine was not equipped with an exhaust manifold and the exhaust pipes ran directly from the cylinders. The airfoil Hirschfelder radiator was mounted in the center of the upper wing. It featured a distinctive filler and a fence-like condensed vapor tank. The bottom surface of the cooler slightly protruded from the wing. Flow of the cooling liquid was regulated by a centrifugal pump. An oil cooler was placed in the forward section of the fuselage.

An L.V.G.-built Albatros D.II sporting a varnish-covered fuselage which made it look dark.

as they were fitted with the Hedtke synchronizing gear (the D.V and D.Va carried the Semmler synchronizer). Ammunition was belt-fed, with 500 rounds per gun. In the cockpit, triggers on the control stick were connected by Bowden cables with the actual gun triggers. The pilot could choose to fire one or both machine guns. The fighter armament weighed 48 kg. German pilots also received a flare gun and 5 rounds, all fitted on either side of the fuselage. The idea was copied by the Austro-Hungarians who frequently placed the gun and ammunition diagonally on the upper wing to make it easily accessible from the cockpit.

The Albatros D.III (Oef) was in turn armed with twin Schwarzlose M16R 8 mm machine guns capable of firing 560-580 rounds per minute[32] or the twin Steyr 7/12 8 mm. Both types were belt-fed with 500 rounds each. Air cooling was preferred, but some examples (e.g. 153.181) sported liquid cooling systems, though such refinements had a negative impact on the fighter's weight. Like their German counterparts, the Oeffag works mounted the guns in front of the cockpit. Their barrels received steel tube extensions that penetrated through the engine block down to fire ports.

There were two methods of mounting the fighter's offensive armament – in the fuselage or externally. The latter was preferred by the pilots as they could re-cock the guns if they had jammed. The Priesel synchronizing gear allowed to shoot though the propeller arc. In the cockpit, triggers on the control stick were connected by Bowden cables with the actual gun triggers. The Oeffag armament solution had one serious deficiency – the Schwarzlose had a lower rate of fire than the German LMG 08/15 as the Priesel synchronizer was of poor quality. Many examples would be plagued with its malfunctions, jamming and poor synchronizing as the propeller was often shot away.

The fuel tank was between the engine and the cockpit and like in the German original it could store 80 l. However the reserve tank was moved to the center section of the upper wing. Oil was stored in an 8 l tank located under the engine.

The armament of the Albatros D.III comprised of twin LMG Spandau 8/15 7.92 mm machine guns mounted in front of the cockpit on the fuselage. With that arrangement pilots had access to their breech blocks and were able to re-cock them should they jam. The guns fired through the propeller arc

The Albatros in Combat

Plans for reorganizing the German air service were drawn up at the turn of June and July 1916 in Charleville with active support from Oswald Böelcke. On August 10 Feldflugchef ordered that *Jagdstaffels* (Jasta) dedicated to engaging enemy planes and observation balloons be established. Their core was to come from the existing *Kampfeinsitzer-Kommandos* (KEKs). The order included also organization

Albatros D.III (OAW) from Jasta 39, serial unknown. It was piloted by Obltn. Josef Leoser. The fighter was painted in white and red stripes. The other aircraft also sports stripes perpendicular to the centerline.

guidelines for the new outfit: a Jagdstaffel fighter squadron was to be composed of 14 single-seat fighters. The newly set up units were to win air superiority for the 1st and 2nd *Armees* preparing for an offensive over the Somme River.

The 1st *Armee* saw three *Jagdstaffels* formed.

On August 22, 1916 Jagdstaffel 1 was established at Berthincourt incorporating the personnel of KEK-Nord and Armee Flug Park[33] 1. Command was given to Hptm. Zander. In its ranks, the unit had such pilots as Lt. Kurt Wintgens who at that time had scored 13 kills and was awarded the Pour le Mérite[34] - the highest decoration for combat valor. By the time of his death on September 25, he had shot down 6 British planes.

On August 27 Berthincourt saw Jagstaffel 2 come to being under Hptm. Oswald Böelcke, who had already achieved 19 air victories and was awarded the Pour le Mérite.

August 21, was the day KEK-Verdun was transformed into Jagdstaffel 5 led by Oblt Hans Beer.

Further three *Jasta*s – 3, 4 and 6 were formed with the 2nd Armee.

As all the *Jasta*s were set up on the basis of existing *Kampfeinsitzerstaffel*s they incorporated their equipment, mainly the Fokker E monoplanes and a small number of D-class Fokker D.I and D.IIIs and Halberstadt D.IIIs and D.Vs.

At this point a definition of the air victory, *Kanone*, exercised by the German air service must be explained. A kill was credited to a pilot who in combat contributed to destroying an enemy airplane or observation balloon by making it hit the ground or burn, though the enemy plane did not necessarily have to crash. The kill had to be confirmed by an independent witness, preferably one who had watched the fight from the ground, or by collected debris. The latter required the enemy plane to crash behind friendly lines. The requirement to prove all victories forced the pilots to land at the wreckage to collect the evidence – skin fragments containing the serial were the most desired. If the enemy was attacked by more than one pilot the kill went to the pilot who contributed the most to the victory. No partial or probable scores were kept. If no one could be credited with a complete kill, it went to the whole *Jasta*. That can be best explained with a history of the first kill scored by Lt. Kurt Wintegens. When flying a Fokker E.I 5/15 he destroyed a French Morane L from MS48[35] on June 1, 1915. He was not credited with the victory and the first individual kill on a Fokker E.I over a French aircraft went to Max Immelman.

A similar rule was exercised by the French but they accepted probable victories a pilot could not prove.

An Albatros D.III (OAW), serial unknown, with stripes on the fuselage.

Albatros D.II(Oef) 53.11 from Flik 24 at the Perigne airfield in June 1917. While flying this aircraft Julius Kowalczik scored his first kill. The black nose, wheels and struts constituted the squadron markings of Flik 24.

The Austro-Hungarian air service lived by the principle that whoever contributed to defeating an enemy plane or observation balloon was credited with a victory. It was not necessary to destroy the target, it was enough to force it to land. In the case of two-seaters, a victory could be credited to a pilot and his observer, regardless of who actually scored the kill. If a larger number of pilots went after the victim, the kill could be awarded to not one, but two pilots who had been the closest to the target. The ace status was assumed by an airman who had had five kills, counted the same way, regardless of the airman's position in the flight crew.

A critical factor for promoting aerial heroes, the aces of the skies, was the unquestionable quagmire of the trench warfare on the front. The warring nations and foot soldiers in the trenches alike needed stories of heroes who defeat the enemy. For that reason Germany published a variety of postcards showing for instance such aces like Max Immelman, Boelcke or Richthofen.

Of the units discussed above the war record of Jasta 2 is worth a closer presentation.

The war-fighting hardware of the unit comprised two Fokker D.IIIs and an Albatros D.I (426/16) that had been delivered in late August[36]. It was enough to fly just a few training sorties to see that the Albatros outclassed the Fokker. By September.16 Jasta 2 had received 5 Albatros D.Is (384/16, 390/16, 391/16, 426/16, 427/16) and one Albatros D.II[37] (386/16). Although the unit at its full strength was expected to field 14 fighter aircraft, Jasta 2 had only nine. The unit's first victory was scored on September 2 by Hptm. Oswald Boelcke flying a Fokker D.III (352/16). It was Boelcke's 20th kill. During the following 15 days he shot down 7 British planes.

Böelcke developed a dogfight tactic exploiting Albatros' performance – high climb-rate and dive speed. An attack was to follow a fixed pattern: upon seeing the target pilots were to gain altitude advantage and engage from the sun. He taught his colleagues to "try to surprise the enemy, fire when he enters the effective range of your gun." The first kill on an Jasta 2 Albatros D.I (probably on 390/16) was scored on September 16, 1916 by Lt. R. Otto Höne, who intercepted and successfully attacked a British F.E.2b from No. 11 Squadron. In the morning hours of Saturday, September 17 five[38] pilots of Jasta 2 took the Albatros on its maiden combat sortie. At approximately 11:00 they attacked west off Marcoing a British formation of 8 B.E.2s escorted by 6 F.E. 2Bs and followed Böelcke's tactics. Within minutes the Germans shot down four planes. It was on that day that Richthofen scored his first kill. He opened up on a French F.E.2b (serial 7018) from just 10 m. The first burst was accurate enough to kill the observer and mortally wound the pilot. The stricken aircraft crashed near Villers Plouich. Richthofen landed on the site and watched the crew being dragged from the wreckage. That was the first out of impressive 80 victories he would score during the war. While flying in Jasta 2 Manfred von Richthofen downed 16 British aircraft. During that encounter Erwin Böme scored his second victory with assistance from other Jasta 2 pilots – Hans Reimann and Jasta 2's leader Böelcke. The latter scored his 27 kill by shooting down that day an F.E.2b piloted by Cpt. D.B. Grey – commander of the No. 11 Squadron, and Lt. I. Helder, his observer. They safely landed despite a damaged engine. After returning to their home aerodrome Jasta 2 pilots threw a huge party to celebrate the unit's

THE ALBATROS IN COMBAT

fist kill and Erwin Böme's decoration with the Iron Cross 1st Class.

On September 22, 1916 Jasta 2 was transferred to Languicourt and took part in the Battle of the Somme. Until his death on October 28, 1916 Böelcke scored 14 kills flying the Albatros D.II 386/16 and 6 more in a Fokker D.III. He died in a mid-air crash with another Albatros piloted by Erwin Böme who had won his fifth victory 6 days earlier and became an ace. The two pilots collided while attacking the same target. At the time of his death Böelcke had been the top fighter ace with 40 confirmed kills. His loss was mourned by the Germans who had already lost another great pilot – Max Immelman.

Lt. Erwin Böme survived the accident and continued to fly in Jasta 2 destroying 22 enemy aircraft (plus two other he had scored in Kampfstaffel 10 – Kasta 10 – and Jasta 29).

On September 23 von Richthofen won his second victory by defeating a Martinsyde G.100 (7481) over Bapaume. By October 16 the junior pilot had been credited with 5 confirmed and claimed 1 probable kill.

Airmen flying the Albatros were quick in becoming aces. Jasta 2 alone produced 20 aces, including Ltn d R. Erwin Böme, Ltn d R. Otto Walter Höne (6 kills), Max Müller (5 plus 28 in Jasta 28; in November 1917 he took over Jasta 2 and shot down five more planes by January 1918).

After Böelcke's death Jasta 2 was taken over by Oblt. Stefan Kirmaier who had won three victories on a Fokker E.III. While leading the unit he shot down 8 planes before he himself fell victim to a D.H.2l on November 22, 1916.

In late 1916 Jasta 2's victory record was close to 100. On December 12, Emperor Wilhelm issued a decree renaming the unit to Jasta "Böelcke."

In June 1917, Jasta 2 became the home unit for Ltn. Paul Bäumer who had already 3 victories to show for his war record. While piloting Albatroses (serials 4409/17, 4430/17 and 5410/17) by November he had shot down 15 planes. By the end of the war he would score 43 kills.

Jasta 2 saw also another great fighter ace flying among its ranks – Ltn. d R. Verner Voss. Assigned to the unit on November 2, 1916, he scored his first two kills on November 27 downing a British Nieuport 17 (A281) and an F.E. 2b (4915)[39]. By the end of 1916, he had defeated only a single B.E. 2d (5782). The ace title came on Feb. 4, 1917, with his fifth victory over a British B.E. 2d (5927). His record continued to grow as by April 7 he had dispatched 24 enemy planes. The following day he was awarded the Pour le Méritte. By May 28, he had scored five more kills and was given command over Jasta 5. There he continued to fly the Albatros and shot down further six planes. He flew a D.III with two personal insignias – a white swastika surrounded by a green laurel wreath and a red heart. Upon a request of Manfred von Richthofen – the commanding officer of the 1st Air Regiment (JG 1) – Voss was transferred to Jasta 10 equipped with the Pfalze D.III. Flying the new aircraft he won three more victories before transitioning to a Fokker Dr.I. Though the change helped him defeat 14 enemy planes, the triplane would turn out to be his last aircraft. He scored the last kill on September 23, 1917, the day of his death. Outnumbered, he engaged in an uneven battle with a group of S.E. 5as from No.

Name	Victories Won Flying the Albatros	Unit – Jasta	Total Victories Won
Manfred von Richthofen	57	2, 11, JG 1	80
Heirich Gontermann	39 (17 balloons)	5, 15	39
Max Müller	36	2, 28	36
Verner Voss	34	2, 5	48
Kurt Wolf	33	11, 29	33
Karl Emil Schäfer	29	11, 28	30
Fritz Röth	28 (20 balloons)	16b	28
Heinrich Claudius Kroll	28	9, 24s	33
Fritz Bernert	27	2	27
Kurt Wüsthoff	26	4	27
Otto Könnecke	25	25, 5	35
Eduard Ritter von Dostler	24	34, 6	26
Lothar von Richthofen	24	11	40
Bruno Loerzer	23	26, JG 3	44
Ernst Udet	23	15, 37, 11, 4	62
Adolf Ritter von Tutschek	23	2, 12	27
Paul Bäumer	22	2	43
Rudolf Berthold	21	4, 14, 18, JG 2	44
Hans Ritter von Adam	21	6	21
Friedrich Altemeier	21	24s	21

Table 1. Fifteen Great Albatros Aces

34   www.kagero.pl

September 1917. FP. Ltn. Szepessy-Sokol from Flik 3 takes off in his Albatros D.II(Oef) 53.02 for his second victory at the Russian Front. The white square for the fuselage cross in unusual.

56 Squadron, piloted by Mc Cudden, Rhus-Davis, Barlow Muspratt, Croynyn Bowman and Childlaw-Roberts among others. During a ten-minute dogfight he managed to fire on all opponents, but was then hit by Lt. Arthur Rhys-Davis and crashed. When James McCudden (57 kills) was writing his wartime memoirs, he recalled Voss: "His flying was wonderful, his courage magnificent and in my opinion he is the bravest German airman whom it has been my privilege to see fight."

In late 1916 thirty two *Jagdstaffels* were formed at the Western Front while the Eastern Front saw only one – Jasta 25[40] – that was successively receiving Al-

batros D.Is, D.IIs and D.IIIs. In December the *Jasta*s had 39 Albatros D.Is and 214 D.IIs (approximately 9 Albatroses per Jasta).

In January 1917 frontline units began to receive the Albatros D.III that would prove to be the best fighter of the Western Front. All famous German pilots took it into combat, Manfred von Richthofen among them. His Albatros war record included 24 victories won on the D.II, 25 on the D.III and 8 on the D.V, 57 total. But it was the D.V that put Richthofen on the receiving end of Allied fighter firepower. When attacking a British F.E. 2b from No. 20 Squadron on July 16, 1917, its observer[41] 2nd Lt. A.E. Woolbridge fired at the approaching fighter from the range of 300 m and wounded its pilot in the head. The German ace was rendered temporarily incapacitated, deaf and blind. He managed to turn off the engine. After descending to 800 m, his sight returned. As Richthofen later recalled, he had noticed two Albatroses covering[42] him on the way back. Eventually, he safely landed and was hospitalized for some time at the 76th Field Hospital at Courtrai.

The list of other German elite fighter pilots who flew the Albatros was long, therefore just the most famous names are mentioned here: Ernst Udet, Kurt Wüsthoff, Kurt Wolf, Herman Göering, Eduard von Schleich, Verner Voss, Lothar von Richthofen, Hans Joahim Buddecke, Rudolf Berthold, Alfred Lentz, Heinrich Claudius Kroll[43].

In the course of war over 350 German pilots enjoying the 'ace' status awarded after scoring 5 kills won their fame flying the Albatros. Amidst them 29

An Albatros D.III(Oef) 53.24 from Fliegerdetachment Nikitsch operating on the Romanian Front in June 1917. Black wing tips suggest the official supplementary markings for the Romanian Front.

were awarded the highest German medal, the Blue Max Pour le Méritte. Initially the distinction was awarded after 8 victories, but later on the number was increased to 30.

Good tactics and superb performance of the Albatros allowed the Germans to inflict heavy losses on the Allies with peak activity in April 1917. The British called it the Bloody April. Led by Manfred von Richthofen, Jasta 11 alone had won 89 victories by the end of the month.

Victories won by German pilots in the spring 1917 were possible due largely to skillful staff of the air service capable of concentrating fighter squadrons and securing tactical superiority on designated front-line sectors. Pilot training[44] and aggressive tactics was critical as well. The latter was possible due to outstanding performance of the Albatros which made the aircraft superior to anything the Allies could put in the air. During the Allied offensive at Arras the British had amassed 754 aircraft including 385 fighters while Germany could only counter with 264 and 114, respectively. Despite the disproportions, by the end of the month it was the British who had lost 245 planes and 319 airmen (pilots and observers), i.e. a third of their aircrews fighting in France.

For the German pilots it was not the enemy aircraft but the observation balloons that posed the greatest challenge. Stationary, sluggish and easy target as they might have been, they were formidable opponents to take on. Balloons were defended by anti-aircraft batteries surrounding the site, enemy fighters patrolling the area to drive off any attackers, balloon observers also often took machine guns for self-defense, not to mention the recovery winch mechanism that allowed ground personnel to pull the balloon down within just a few minutes. However, it was the hydrogen filling the balloon that the pilots feared most. If its fabric envelope was punctured, the gas would escape and mix with air to produce a highly explosive mixture. If for instance phosphorus rounds were fired, the mixture would ignite and blow up. Unless the fighter kept well clear of its blazing prey, it would have been consumed by the conflagration. A special tactic was required to take balloon crews by surprise. Soon some German pilots became 'Kanone' balloon-busters, e.g. Fritz Röth, Heinrich Gontermann, Carl Schelgel, Oskar Hennrich, Fritz Friedrichs, Friedrich Höhn and Max Näther. Röth who piloted the Albatros became famous for his multiple-balloon-kill-day on May 29, 1918. During one ninety-minute sortie he single-handedly destroyed 5 observation balloons in the Dixmiude-Poperinghe-Hazebrouck sector while outmaneuvering a French Spad trying to fend him off. As he later recalled, he had fired 20 phosphorous and 20 'K' rounds at each target. Two of those were

Albatros D.III(Oef) 53.30 from Flik 55J. It was piloted by Austro-Hungary's second top-scoring ace FP. Offstv. Julius Arigi.

Albatros D.III(Oef) 53.37 from Flik 48. The red nose, wheels and struts constituted Flik 48's markings which shared the Perigine airfield with Stabsfeldw. Josef Kiss Flik 24. October 1917. This example received a refeinement unusual for Austro-Hungarian-built Albatroses – a German strenthening of the lower wings by additional small struts. Next to the airplane is Stabsfeldwebel Josef Kiss, Austria-Hungary's fifth top scoring fighter pilot.

Albatros D.III(Oef) 153.109 assigned to Waffenversuchs-flik based at Fischamend where it was used for testing aerial guns and synchronizers.

British, three Belgian. Tables turned on him when he encountered a D.H. 9 from No. 108 Squadron. Röth brought the enemy down but was shot in both legs, which put an end to his remarkable career. That was his 28th victory and 82nd for Jasta 16b[45].

As early as the autumn 1916 and spring 1917 pilots began to paint their aircraft in provocative colors to show the enemy who they were dealing with. Allegedly Ltn. D R. Diether Collin from Jasta 2 was the first to start the practice with his light grey and green Albatros (probably 384/16). The plane was then taken over by Prinz Friedrich Karl of Prussia who commanded Fl Abt (A) 258 and only seldom flew a D.I in Jasta 2.

After his 40th victory in April 1917, Manfred von Richthofen ordered that his D.III be painted red, hence giving birth to his nick-name 'Rote Baron', the Red Baron. Other pilots followed. Allmoenröder was recognized by his white-nosed, all-red fighter,

Ernst Udet and Teodor Rumpl from Jasta 23b had some of their fighters painted red. Such was the color also of Godwin Brumowski's D.III (Oef). Black panted Albatroses belonged to Ernst Udet, Eduard von Schleich and Lt. Bertrab, Josef Jacobs, Otto Kisesenberth, Kurt Schonfelder, Adolf Ritter von Tutschek and Joachim von Bertrab. Stripes were characteristic for Helmut Dilthey, Theodor Rumpl and Bruno Loerzer. The British pilots believed in a legend about a pink Albatros nick-named the "Pink Lady" flown by a woman avenging her dead husband.

With the Allies winning back air superiority the German air service was forced to form up a unit larger than the Jagdstaffel to counter the emerging threat. On June 23, 1917, Gen. Ernst von Höppner, head of Kommandieren General der Luftstreitkrdfte (Kogenluft for short) issued Order No. 5834-1:

"Squadrons 4th, 6th, 10th, 11th are to form up Jagdgeschwader 1 (JG 1 – the 1st Fighter Regiment).

The Regiment is to be an independent unit dedicated to winning and sustaining air supremacy at front sectors of critical importance."

Its command was given to Rtm. Manfred von Richthofen. A subsequent JG, JG 2 incorporating Jastas 12, 13, 15 and 19 was established on Feb. 2, 1918. Hptm Adolf Ritter von Tutschek, a famous Bavarian ace, was put in charge and after his death the job went to Hptm Rudolf Berthold[46]. Each JG was subordinate to an Armee Oberkommando, AOK (Armee HQ). Theoretically, a JG was to be composed of 56 fighters. Further JG regiments were set up in the spring and summer 1918. Other organization improvements included building a large network of observation posts to alarm JG 1 leaders about enemy air activity over the frontline. Once planes were spotted individual Jastas were scrambled. That allowed Germany to win local air superiority and effectively inflict losses on the Allies.

The Albatros fighters played an important role in the aerial combat of the Great War. They were the workhorse of the German air service from the autumn of 1916 to the summer of 1918. During that period the Albatros became the most popular plane in the German air service. The type was used on all fronts not only by the Germans but the Turks, Austro-Hungarians and Bulgarians as well. However, thoughts of the First World War preserved only the Fokkers, particularly the Dr. I and D.VII. Perhaps this has been caused by the U.S.-made films about the conflict or this just a merit to be credited to the great marketing campaign Anthony Fokker put up.

Most books about that period link Richthofen with the Fokker Dr.I, the aircraft he flew to his end. However, it was the Albatros family that enabled him to score 57 kills, i.e. 71.25% of his total number of victories. While flying the Fokker Dr.I he scored only 17 kills – 21.25% of the total, and 6 (7.5%) in March 1917 on a Halberstadt D.II.

The Albatros allowed the Germans to enjoy air superiority, with particular emphasis on local domination, until the Allies introduced in large numbers the

Table 2. Number of fighter aircraft manufactured in 1916-1918		
Aircraft	Number Built	Country
Albatros D.I, D.II, D.III, D.V and D.Va	3730	Germany
Fokker Dr.I	320	Germany
Fokker D.VII	861	Germany
Fokker E.V and D.VIII	381	Germany
Pfalz D.III and D.IIIa	1000	Germany
SSW D.III and D.IV	212	Germany
Sopwith Triplane	150	Great Britain
Sopwith Pup	1770	Great Britain
Sopwith Camel	5490	Great Britain
Sopwith Snipe	497	Great Britain
Sopwith Dolphin	1500	Great Britain
S.E.5 and S.E.5a	5205	Great Britain
Bristol F.2B	5200	Great Britain
Nieuports	7200	France
Spad 7 and 13	11972	France
Hanriot HD.1	956	France

Spad 13, S.E 5, S.E. 5a, F.2B and a range of Sopwith fighters including the Camel and Bristol. Eventually, they outnumbered the Germans 6:1 and grew increasingly effective in defeating German aircraft, fighters in particular. This is best illustrated by the table comparing the number of Albatroses built in Germany in comparison to Entente's principal fighters.

The records of both German and Allied victories show that a large percentage of kills scored by the Germans and French was against reconnaissance and light bomber two-seaters, as well as the observation balloons. Those targets enjoyed immediate top priority in combat. Moreover, they were easier to defeat in dogfight than Allied fighter peers.

On the other hand, the war record of Royal Flying Corps (RFC) and Royal Navy Air Service (RNAS) prove that British pilots were more keen on tackling German fighters and the Albatros in particular. The British inverted their target priority list to first engage enemy fighters and only then go after

Machine guns fitted on the D.III (Oef) that was piloted by FP. Hpt. Godwin Brumowski.

Albatros D.III (Oef) 153.07 in natural finish.

Table 3. Albatros Killers				
Name	Albatros Kills/ Total Kills	Aircraft Flown	Unit	Nationality
Collishaw Raymond	29/60	Camel	10N, 203	RNAS/RFC/Canada
Fullard Philip	25/40	Nieuports	1	RFC
Bowman Geofrey	19/32	S.E.5a	56	RFC
Richard A. Maybery	19/21	S.E.5a	56	RFC/Wales
Geaofrey H. Bowman	17/32	S.E.5a	56	RFC
Jordan William L.	15/39	Camel	8N, 201	RNAS/RFC/South Africa
McCudden James	14/57	Sopwith Pup, S.E. 5a	56	RFC
Worlet Henry	14/35	Camel	24,43	RFC
Cowell John	14/16	F.E.2d	20	RFC
Kinkead Samuel M.	14/35	Camel	3 W,1 N.,47, 201	RNAS/RFC/South Africa
Carpenter Peter	14/24	Camel	45, 66	RFC/Wales
Beauchamp-Proctor Andrew F. W.	13/54	S.E.5a	84	RFC/South Africa
Mannock Edward	12/61	Nieuport, Se 5a	40,70,85	RFC
Wiliam A. Bishop	12/72	S.E.5a	60	RFC
Gass Charles	12/39	Bristol F.2B	22	RFC
Beaver Wilfried	12/19	Bristol F2B	20	RFC/USA
McElroy George E. H.	11/47	Se 5a	40 i 24	RFC/Ireland
Gilmour John Ingles	10/39	Martinside, Camel		RFC/Scotland
Thompson Samuel	8/30	Bristol F.2B	22	RFC
Ball Albert	7/44	S.E.5a	56	RFC
Iaccaci Paul	6/17	Bristol F.2B	20	RFC/USA
Guynemer Georges	5/53	Spad 7 C1, 13	N3/SPA	France
De Turenne Armand	5/15	Nieuport, Spad	N48-Spa 12	France

recce planes or observation balloons. At the top of Allied fighter pilot list there are four who mainly flew No. 56. Squadron's S.E.5a. In many respects the type was better than the Albatros but offered poorer armament. British pilots could escape volleys of fire from the Albatros by diving and out-running the enemy who, if elected to give chase, would see its lower wing flatter and tear away. Some German pilots excelled in shooting the S.E.5a, like Ltn Otto Könecke from Jasta 5a who flying an Albatros D.Va dispatched 25 plus 10 on other fighters.

The table shows that amidst the Albatros killers there were also flight crews of the Bristol F.2b two-seat fighter.

Despite the fact that the Albatros was the mainstay of Jastas, the number of victories won by their pilots slightly dropped in the spring and summer 1918. Though less effective, Albatros pilots were rushed into combat during the German offensive launched in March 1918. The following table shows the number of Albatroses deployed in individual months of service.

On April 30, 90 Jastas fielded 928 Albatros D.Vas (47.6% of the whole fighter force) 131 D.Vs (6.7%), and 174 D.IIIs (8.9%), which totaled 63.2% of all fighters. The second type so broadly deployed was the Pfalze D.III with 433 examples (22.2%). After April 30, the number of Albatroses began to decline rapidly giving way to the Fokker D.VII that got top priority and even the Albatros plant set up its license production at the cost of its indigenous designs output. The Fokker reigned over the frontlines throughout the summer and autumn 1918, although the Albatros still served in some Jastas.

Table 4. The number of Albatroses at the front					
Month/Year	D.I	D.II	D.III	D.V	D.Va
September/1916	6	1			
November/1916	50	28			
January/1917	39	214	13		
March/1917	28	212	137		
May/1917	20	154	327		
July/1917*	17	90	303	216	
September/1917	12	44	385	424	
November/1917	9	11	446	526	53
January/1918	8	6	423	513	186
March/1918	5	2	357	250	475
May/1918**	6	2	174	131	986
July/1918	1	2	82	91	604
September/1918	3	2	52	20	307

* The first two Fokker Dr.Is were assigned to JG 1
** The first Fokker D.VII were assigned to Jasta 10 from JG 1

Flik 2D's Albatros D.III (Oef) 153.95 named "RIT-TA" (painted on port side) was flown without a spinner. "RITTA" was crashed by Oblt. Fritz Losert from Flik 30.

The Albatros D.II (Oef) and D.III (Oef) began their military service in the Austro-Hungarian air arm once FLARS (Fliegerarsenal) air service inspectorate cleared them for combat units. The D.II (Oef) was accepted on May 4, 1917, the D.III (Oef) followed late the same month. The first examples reached frontline units in early June. They were assigned to *Flik*s 19, 24, 32, 33, 35, 40, 42, 46, 47 and 48. Each unit initially received only one Albatros to escort reconnaissance aircraft. On June 19, 1917 Flik 24's Fw. Julius Kowalczik flying a D.II (Oef) (serial no. 53.02) scored the type's first kill by shooting down an Italian Caudron two-seater from 50[A] Squadriglia over Cima Maora in the Val Sugana valley. It opened a long record

of victories Austro-Hungarian pilots would win flying Austrian-produced Albatros. For the pilot it was the last confirmed kill[47] earning him the title of an ace.

February 1917 saw the formation of purebred fighter units resembling the German *Jastas*. The first was Flik 41J[47], command of which was given to a Wadowice-born Hauptman Godwin Brumowski who by that time had 5 credited kills. The unit became the best fighter unit in the entire Austro-Hungarian air service with many top-scoring k.u.k. LFT pilots serving there at some point: Franciszek Linke Crawford (27 kills), Kurt Gruber (11), Karl Kaszala (8), Friederich Navratil (10), Julius Aurigi (32) and Beno Fiala (28).

On May 10, 1917 Godwin Brumowski flying a Brandenburg D.I (serial 28.10) won the unit's first kill

Albatros D.III(Oef)153.112 was the first example with rounded nose and probably the only one with hand painted lozenge camouflage similar to the German pattern.

Interior of an Albatros D.II (Oef) cockpit. One machine gun is completely embedded in the fuselage.

ranked third among Austro-Hungarian aces. Starting from the position of an observer on July 28, 1914, he was assigned to Fliegerkompanie 1 at the Galician Front. He flew the Aviatik B.I 'Durch' among other aircraft. With technical background, he pioneered the use of plane-mounted radios in the Austro-Hungarian air service. On June 6 and 13, 1915 he scored two unconfirmed kills. He had to wait until Apr. 29, 1916, to be officially credited in the records of Flik 19 fighting on the Italian Front. Five days later he flew a sortie with Flik 19's commander FP. Lt. Ludwig Heyrowski serving as his pilot and shot down an Italian M.4 airship. After graduating from a flight school he was reassigned to Flik 41J and then to Flik 12D. There he scored seven kills in a Hansa Brandenburg D.I. In November 1917, he was sent to Flik 56J, where flying a D.III (Oef) 153.77 he defeated his 10th opponent. Promoted in January 1918 to lead Flik 56J he continued to fly a D.III and by August 20 he had scored 20 kills. The last to fall victim to his gun was an S.V.A.5 south of Papadopoli Island near Cissalto. After World War One he took a job in Poland as a manager of a Junkers workshop at the Aerolot Polish Airlines in Warsaw in 1928-1929.

The Poles, who constituted about 10% of Austro-Hugary's population, were drafted to the military including the air service. They served as observers, pilots and mechanics in the *Flik*s. Some were reassigned from the Legions to later become the core of the future Polish air service. Leutnants Marian Gaweł[48] (1 kill) and Henryk Szeliga served in Flik 41J from June 1917. There was also a large number of Polish servicemen who were involved in the Albatros war.

Flik 61J became the unit of Leutnant in der Reserve Eugeniusz Roland, Antoni Skislewicz and Henryk Skoczdopole who flew a red-nosed Albatros D.III (Oef) serial no. 153.217. He was shot down on July

(it was his 6th). The first victory in a D.III (Oef) 153.45 was over an Italian observation balloon he downed over the Shobba Estuary. While flying the Albatros D.III (Oef) 153.45, 153.42 and 152.209 Brumowski destroyed 14 enemy planes and crash-landed combat-damaged 153.45 and 153.52.

The following table lists the names of Austro-Hungarian aces who scored 5 or more victories while flying the Albatros D.III (Oef).

The history of the Albatros D.III (Oef) aces requires a closer look at the achievements of FP. Oblt. Benno Fiala Ritter (Baron) von Fernbrugg who

Pilot	Victories		Flik No.	Pilot's Albatros serial no.
	Albatros	Total		
Benno Fiala Ritter von Fernbrugg	19	28	51J	153.77,153.128,153.270,153.155
Franz Gräser	16	18	42J, 61J	153.13, 153.44,153.61,153.106, 153.111
Eugen Bönsch	16	16	51J	53.57, 153.35, 253.37
Godwin Brumowski	14	35	41J	153.06, 153.45, 153.52, 153.209
Julius Arigi	13	32	55J	153.15,153.36,153.80
Friedrich Navratil	10	10	41J i 3J	253.07
Josef Kiss	12	19	55J	153.17, 153.47, 153.87
Stefan Fejes	11	16	51J	153.128, 153.132, 153.142, 253.54
Ernst Strohschneider	10	15	42J, 61J	153.111, 153.119
Franz Rudorfer	10	11	51J	153.141, 253.122, 253.124
Franz Linke Crawford	9	27	41J	153.04,153.11,153.16
Georg Kenzian	7	9	55J	153.27, 153.107
Josef von Maier	7	7	55J	153.64
Franz Peter	6	6	3J	253.04, 253.05
Alexander Kasza	5	6	55J	153.19, 153.40
Franz Lahner	5	5	55J	153.19,153.70, 153.158

*pilot participated in a kill

Albatros D.III (Oef) machine guns were fully embedded in the fuselage. The visible machine-gun blast tubes go underneath exhaust pipes.

5, 1917, in a D.III (Oef) 153.181 during a duel with two Spads.

In Flik 9J Leutnant Stanisław Bogusz piloted Albatros D.III (Oef)s, serials 53.38 and 153.240. The unit was led for a short time by Oberleutnant in der Reserve Stefan Stec.

Among the personnel of another Flik – 42J – were Leutnant in der Reserve Zygmunt Kostrzewski[49] and Zugs. Jan Ryba who was killed on August 28, 1918 in a D.III (Oef), serial 253.69, over Casa Musile.

On May 2, 1918, FLik 69J's Leutnant in der Reserve Kajetan Kosiński flying an Albators D.III (Oef) 153.176 encountered three Sopwith Camels from RFC's No. 66 Squadron and was shot down by Canadian Lt. Gerard Alfred Birks (with 12 victories).

Flik 3J was initially commanded by Hpt. Zwierzina who handed it over on June 9, 1918 to FP. Ober-

leutnant Friedrich Navratil[50]. In the spring 1918[51], FP. Oberleutnant in der Reserve[52] Stefan Stec[53], Stanisław Maria Tomicki from Tomice (he obtained the pilot's certificate no. 966 on January 6, 1918) and Michał Solski joined the unit. It was originally a reconnaissance unit that in September 1917 used an Albatros D.II (Oef) serial 53.11 for escort purposes. It was piloted by Hungarian FP. Oberleutnant Rudolf Szepessy-Sokol[54] credited with 5 kills.

The combat records of Flik 3 stationed at the Romagnano aerodrome deserve a closer look.

The Flik's first victory was scored on June 28, 1917 by FP. Oblt. Friederich Navratil. Flying an Albatros D.III (Oef) serial 153.198 he engaged two Italian Spads in a dogfight over Zugna-Ospendaletto and destroyed them both. One of the most successful engagements was a fight between Navratil, Stec and

Albatros D.III (Oef) 253.01 was the first D.III (Oef) example to be fitted with the new 220 hp (161 kW) powerplant.

Aircraft fitted with raised Schwarzlose M 7/17 guns. Note the machine-gun blast tubes under the exhaust pipes.

FP. Oblt. Franz Peter and Hanriot HD 1s from the 72ᴬ Squadriglia near Lake Garda in the Val de Concei valley on July 16. Without suffering any losses they shot down one and forced two Hanriots to land. Stec scored his second kill while Peter was credited with two more enemy planes destroyed. On July 23, Navratil destroyed a Bristol F2B from RFC's No. 139 Squadron over the Matarello railroad station.

This kill made him an ace. Franz Peter's third victory was on August 4, south of Aldeno where he killed Flt. Sergente Arrigoni flying an SVA V. August 10 was a lucky day for Stec who in an Albatros D. III (Oef) downed an aircraft of unknown type. This was the last confirmed kill of this pilot in the Great War. Franz Peter continued to wreak havoc on the enemy and on August 20, when flying a D.III (Oef)

Albatros D.III (Oef) serial 53.27 that was piloted by Lt. i D R. Franz Gräser of Flik 43J stationed at Maria la Longa near Trieste. Some sources mistakenly assigned it to Bumowski or Linienschiffsleutnant Gottfrid Banflied from K.u.K. Seeflugwesen. In fact Banflied, standing in the center, had flown a recce sortie in it while visiting Flik 42J. The plane sported green top surfaces with spirals and identically painted wheel hubs. Other surfaces retained the natural finish. Noteworthy is the lack of the spinner.

THE ALBATROS IN COMBAT

Hpt. Brumowski's personal insignia.

serial 253.04, he dispatched a two-seat reconnaissance plane from 134ᴬ Squadriglia.

August was a lucky month for Navratil who scored 5 more kills, all in a D.III (Oef) 253.06. On September 17 Franz Peter destroyed an Italian SIA from 134ᴬ Squadriglia near Borcola Pas on Monta Pasubio. Almost three weeks later on October 7, after a tough dogfight he shot down a Sopwith Camel from No. 66 Squadron between Trento and Pergine. Zugs. Kurt Steidl in a D.III (Oef) 253.120 participated in the fight and was eventually credited with the kill.

In the course of war Flik 3 J lost five D.III (Oef)s. The first one, serial 153.249, was destroyed on July 14, 1918, when Stf. Sgt. Michał Solski fighting with three Sopwith Camels from No. 45 Squadron was shot down between Asiago and Arsiero.

On August 31, the unit suffered the most severe losses of the war. In the morning 6 Albatros fighters took off for a patrol. Over Zugna a British F.2B was detected at 4500 m. Navratil and Stec broke off to pursue the target and dispatched it about 7 km behind Italian lines. Both pilots in turns attacked the British, but it was Navratil who was credited with the kill. In the meantime, the now 4-plane formation continued the patrol and at 9:45 it was ambushed by three Camels from RFC's No. 45 Squadron. Completely surprised they stood no chance against the Brits and within minutes all four Albatroses were down. J. Cottie shot two planes and his colleague M.R. James further two, including one wearing a white and red checkerboard– pilot's personal emblem. Engulfed in flames, it crashed near Roccolo-Bagathini. Its pilot Stanisław Tomicki was killed. He was buried in Arsiero. Two other pilots were killed: Jaroslav Kubelik and Josef Pürer (who had graduated from flight school on July 11). The fourth one – Otto Forster was severely wounded and hospitalized. Upon their return Navratil and Stec failed to find any of their colleagues from the ill-fated patrol flight. An investigation that followed determined a "lack of air discipline." Stec's and Peter's friendship made the latter enlist in the Polish air service and successfully apply for Polish citizenship, which he cherished to the end of his days.

Stefan Stec was credited[55] with seven victories, though none had been officially confirmed. As a tidbit, the original record was: "The first one was on June 28, during a flight with Sgt. Otto Firster[56] near Val de Concei, next on August 10 over Monte Passubio, three other on the 18th, 20th and 29th."

On October 21, Navratil crashed an Albatros D.III (Oef) serial 263.06 at his home aerodrome and was severely injured. The plane was written off.

To sum up air operations of Flik 3J, the K.u.K. pilots were highly effective. For the loss of five of their own, they destroyed over 20 enemy planes.

Contrary to the stereotypical image of the Austro-Hungarian forces, the k.u.k. LFT pilots were an elite group, valiant and brave.

A pair of Albatroses: Hpt.Godwin Brumowski's D.III (Oef) 153.45 with yet another insignia of the pilot and Oblt. Linke Crawford's D.III (Oef) 153.16 with the pilot's second recognition insignia – the hawk. Closer analysis of the picture may suggest that Brumoski's fighter was not painted red. Crawford's was black-nosed. Brumowski and Crawford (in white pants) stand by their planes.

Brumowski's Albatros D.III (Oef) 153.45 with partially burnt skin on the upper right and lower wings (details of the event described in the text). The plane was all-red.

The end of the Great War in November 1918 did not put an end to a number of local conflicts and border clashes that had broken out after October 16, 1918, the day the Austro-Hungarian Emperor declared that monarchy's subject nations have the right to self-determination. Austria was consequently embroiled in a dispute with Slovenia and the SHS (Serbia, Croatia and Slovenia) Confederacy over the Carinthia province south of Graz. Hostilities broke out in late 1918 after Austro-Hungary fell apart. An

air detachment formed ad hoc by Volksehr Deutsch-Osterreich took part in the fighting. It was set up in Klagenfurt under Hauptman Julius Yllam. The Klagenfurt-Annabichl aerodrome became the rallying point for individual aircraft detached from Fliks scattered all over Hungary, Bohemia and Slovenia. Nearby airfields were scrounged for airframe and engine spare parts. In December 1918, Kartener Fliegertruppe 2a had 14 aircraft, including three Albatros D.III (Oef)s, known serials 253.132 and 253.185, and

Albatros D.III (Oef) 253.64 that was flown by Stfw. Friedrich Hefty from Flik 42J. The plane had spiral-covered canvas skin and mixed markings combining old-fashioned and 1918 recognition marks. The picture was taken on Aug. 28, 1918 at Pinzano after an unfortunate landing when the right lower wing had been damaged in the process.

Oblt. Navratil's Albatros D.III (Oef) 253.116 in flight.

In the Polish Air Force

As a matter of fact, the first Albatros D.IIs, D.IIIs and D.Vs to enter the Polish Air Force were spoils of war, most of them captured at the Zeppelin Hall in Poznan. One of the machines was an Albatros D-II serial 1765/16 that after refurbishment was donated to the Flight School in Ławica. Por.Pil. Jach was one of the pilots who flew it. Preserved documents[58] list another D-II that after refurbishment was scheduled to be assigned to the 59th Breguet Squadron.

By March 1919, the Wielkopolska air component had had about ten D.IIIs, one D.V and 15 D.Vas (one served as the escape plane for Kpr. Pil. A. Bartkowiak who flew away from Bydgoszcz to Poznań, Por. Pil. Wiktor Lang flew another). Further Albatros D.IIIs were acquired directly from the OAW plant in Piła, two other in Gdańsk.

In 1919, the D.III was in service with Wielkopolska Squadrons. Reconnaissance units received one fighter – either a D.III or Fokker D.VII – assigned with escort duties. Por. Pil. Franciszek Jach from the 1st 'Wielkopolska' Squadron destroyed[59] or damaged an observation balloon. This is how he described this event in his memoirs:

"On May 8, 1919, I received orders to attack a Ukrainian balloon that was frequently appearing in the skies southeast of Przemyśl, near the city of Sambor. The balloon had been fired upon and bombed by planes from the 5th 'Galician' Squadron a number of times already, but no pilot dared to descend that low as the target was well defended. May 9 came with a uniquely clear air. I went to the aerodrome as early as 4 a.m. and waited until 10 for the balloon to show up. It did not. In the afternoon I received a new order: take off and reach the Lwów sector in the evening to monitor any movement on the bridges across the Dniester River near Mikolajów. I immediately set off to the aerodrome about 3 km away from my quarters. There I saw a bullet-riddled Albatros from enemy fire that battered the plane whenever it flew (every hole was marked

a Hansa Brandenburg KD 128.14. The remainder of the component flew various marks of Brandenburg B.I and C.I two-seaters (e.g. 29.90, 369.27, 429.39 and 64.66), Phönixes and Ufags. They flew reconnaissance, liaison, ground attack and bombing sorties against Slovenian positions. Albatros D.III (Oef)s flew escort for the two-seaters.

The SCS confederate air service was made of former Austro-Hungarian servicemen and equipment. Air operations were launched during the battle of Bierbaumer fought December 19-21, 1918. On May 22, 1919, SSgt.[57] Svecz in an Albatros D.III (Oef) was fired upon and forced to land. Pretending to be Italian he fixed the plane and took off but empty fuel tanks forced him to land again near Krainburg. This time pretending to be Yugoslavian he wangled fuel out of a passing driver and resumed the flight. Eventually, he managed to return to his home airfield. In the course of fighting, a Yugoslavian two-seater was shot down on May 30. Hostilities lasted until June 1919. By that time fighters had flown 24 combat sorties. The border conflict was resolved in a plebiscite. Austria retained southern Carinthia, while Italy and Yugoslavia got to share over 500 sq. km. A peace treaty signed in September in St. Germain stipulated that all fighter planes be destroyed. An Allied Committee oversaw the process.

Albatroses D.III (Oef) from Flik 3J at Romagnano airfield. From the right to left : Navratil's 253.06, Stec's 253.117,Navratil's second plane with a different insignia, Peter's 253.116. The leftmost fighter 153.227 was piloted by Fw. Arpad Kurtnecker.

Oblt. Friedrich Navratil in Albatros D.III (Oef) 253.16. The picture well shows how camouflage pattern was painted using a sponge or a swab.

The crash site of Albatros D.III (Oef) 0.20 repaired at the CAW in Warsaw. It featured green top and lateral surfaces, light blue bottom surfaces and struts, metal parts retained their natural finish.

The crash of an Albatros D.III (Oef) in which Sierż. Pil. Emil Mejer was killed on May 5, 1919. Although the aircraft serial is unknown, Mejer's plane was recognized by his arrow-pierced heart insignia. Date of the crash and pilot's name was chalked next to it after the crash.

An Albatros D.III (Oef), serial unknown, probably in natural colors. At the front the Oeffag logo is visible. Its pilot was recognized by his red heart insignia on the fuselage.

with an amaranth and a white circle). Suddenly, at 4 the balloon appeared. It took far too long to start the engine and by then the balloon had already disappeared. I got airborne nonetheless, climbed high to take position that would allow me to attack by surprise from the sun. Though the balloon had already been deflated on the ground lying in front of its hangar I decided to press the attack against all odds and dived towards the target. At close range I opened up from my two machine gun positions and fired up to 150 rounds right on the money. I saw the phosphorus rounds hitting the fabric canopy, but they failed to set it on fire. The machine gun firing phosphorus rounds ceased and the engine began to falter. I noticed that my main fuel tank had been ruptured so I switched to an emergency tank. During my second strike I targeted three machine guns grouped together that had put up barrage fire from the moment I was detected. After my pass the guns fell silent, the crew of the middle one killed, others had fled to seek shelter. I descended so low that the plane was skimming the treetops. The shot-up balloon was right below me. Suddenly, somewhere from the tree line shots were fired. Enemy fire was accurate and my engine started to spatter even more, while my helmet, sleeve and flight jacket earned a few holes. I nursed the fighter as long as I could. When the engine ceased the plane hit a hilltop and without losing momentum slid downhill into a valley. It stopped in barbed wire. I landed in no-man's land, 300 m from the Polish lines and 200 m from Ukrainian trenches."

The Albatros D.II and D.V was used for reconnaissance missions over German-occupied territories.

Most of available planes were used for training and practice at flight schools, primarily at Ławica.

Individual Albatroses were assigned to the 1st, 2nd and 3rd 'Wielkopolska' Squadrons and 3rd, 5th (2 D.Vas), 8th and 9th Reconnaissance Squadrons for escort duties. The Albatros operated on the Wielkopolska, Southern, Lithuanian and Belarusian Fronts and in eastern Małopolska, where they carried out escort, reconnaissance and attack missions, particularly against Semyon Budyonny's cavalry.

One of the Albatros D.Vs acquired in May 1920 in Gdańsk, operated for a short period of time with BDL – Naval Aviation. It was piloted by Ppor. Pil. Adolf Stempkowski.

On September 28, 1919, during an aviation day at the Poznań Ławica aerodrome, a mock dogfight was demonstrated by three D.IIIs, while another D.III (serial 2586/17) piloted by a master pilot Adam Haber-Włyński delivered an acrobatics show.

As early as the assembly stage in the spring of 1920, a number of Albatros D.IIIs received strengthened spars and a bracing pylon linking the lower wing's leading edge and the interplane struts. Design changes were made to allow for additional 100 kg of payload – bombs or extra fuel[60].

Despite those efforts accidents happened when the lower wing separated from the plane (ill-fated 3119/17 and 1926/17). The last mishap was on December 14, 1919 at AOS[61] in Warsaw. During the maiden flight of a CWL D.III serial 0.16, its wings separated

Early November 1919. Flight leaders Corsi and Cooper are pictured next to a D.III (Oef) from the 7th Fighter Squadron. No markings had been painted on the (probably) all-green fuselage.

at 400 m and the plane crashed killing AOS' instructor Sierż. Pil. Jan Szalczewski. A few days later the Air Forces Inspectorate issued order no. 36 decommissioning and permanently grounding all D.IIIs. However, serials 1680/17, 1846/17 and 3218/17 were not scrapped but assigned to the 1st and 3rd Air Regiment. Two were transferred to Advanced Pilot Training School at Grudziądz. The 1846/17 was on roster of the APTS until March 28, 1923. The last Polish Albatros D.V was decommissioned in November 1922.

The Albatros D.III (Oef) in the Polish Air Force

In Małopolska seven aircraft described as Oeffags were captured. Some must have been two-seaters, but some fighters might have been among that number as well. Further 10 D.III (Oef)s (?) were captured in Kongresówka (a nickname of Russian occupied part of Poland). Three of those were rebuilt

The combat-ready 7th Fighter Squadron, here seen at Lvov in December 1919. The foremost plane belonged to Maj. Cedric Flaunt le Roy.

at the Centralne Warsztaty Lotnicze – CWL (Central Aviation Works) in Mokotów and assigned serials 0.20, 0.21 and 0.22. The other seven were also rebuilt rather than refurbished at the 2. Remontowy Park Lotniczy (2nd Air Repair Workshop). These were mostly series 253 examples but an assumption can be made that series 53 and 153 planes were also there. Unfortunately, this cannot be unequivocally substantiated by existing documents, especially that during subsequent overhauls the airframes were upgraded to the 253 series standard with the same bracing as in the original Oeffag series 253. These aircraft were assigned to escadrons and flight schools.

By late 1918, it had become clear that without acquiring new aircraft, fighter types in particular, it would be hard to wage war. Therefore, Polish authorities were keen to accept the first offer that became available. On December 31, 1918 the Austrian Oeffag proposed to sell 100 series 253 Albatros D.III (Oef)s. It was accepted and already on January 13, 1919 the Polish government signed with Oeffag a contract for 12 aircraft. Its terms were beneficial as delivery was planned for completion between 8 and 25 January 1919. Things got complicated when Karoserie Fabrik offered Poland the latest series 85 WKF model powered by the 184 kW (250 hp) engine. To make a sensible choice between the two types, they were subjected to comparative tests at Wiener Neustadt. An Albatros D.III (Oef) 253.224 and WKF 85.04 were sent for final evaluation. Flights were to be carried out by experienced pilots Julius Arigi and Karl Keizar. A mixed Austro-Polish committee was established, composed among others of Kpt. Wierzejewski, Kpt. Zimmerman, Por. Pil. Stefan Stec and engineers Wacławinek and Prawdziwic-Rubczyński.

After the competition the pilots demonstrated flight characteristics of the two types and, following Lt. Stec's significant contribution, the D.III (Oef) was selected. The contractor offered additional 14 D.III (Oef)s along with 15 Heinecke parachutes. They were assigned to the 7th Fighter Squadron (7 Eskadra Myśliwska). On November 22, one of the unit's pilots, Por. Pil. Graves attempted to bail out but he was flying too low for the chute to deploy. Though fatal, this was probably the first parachute bail out in the entire Polish Air Force.

The Oeffag plant faced problems in delivering the contracted planes for reasons beyond its control. The contract could not be completed as there had been no international economic cooperation in place between Poland and Austria. After the requisite agreements were signed on May 10, 1919, the D.III (Oef)s were delivered.

In July 1919 26[62] series 253 Albatros D.III (Oef)s[63] arrived at the Mokotów aerodrome. As Oeffag was keen to continue the sales of the type the third fighter contract was signed in Vienna. Twelve new aircraft were delivered on October 20, 1919. In Austria Poland acquired 38 series 253 Albatros D.III (Oef)s (253.212-253.230, 353.232, 253.234-253.239, 253.243-253.248, 253.251-257).

Along with the aircraft, 82 Austro Daimler engines producing 136 and 165 kW (185 and 225 hp respectively) and a variety of parts required for future overhauls were secured.

Final assembly of the D.III (Oef)s was conducted at the CWL. Eight[64] completed machines were sent in August to Lwów where they were assigned to the 7th Fighter Squadron with subsequent examples following in October and November[65] 1919 until the unit reached its full strength. By the end of the year 13 fighters had been delivered to the 7th FS. It suffered its first loss on November 22, 1919, when Por. Pil. Edmund Graves flying 253.222 (tactical no. 5) crashed during the first commemoration of the Lwów campaign. This was the 7th FS's first loss since American airmen had joined it.

In March 1920, 11 Oeffag D.IIIs were sent to the Poznań-based 13th Fighter Squadron (13 Eskadra Myśliwska). Individual aircraft were assigned to high ranking commanding officers for personal usage, e.g. the 253.214 to the 5th Squadron's Leader

Albatros D.III (Oef)s of the 7th Fighter Squadron. The no. 8 plane wears the blue markings of the 'Pułaski' flight.

A red-nosed Albatros D.III (Oef), No. 3 from the 'Kościuszko' flight. The plane piloted by Lt. Chess crashed on January 28 at Lewandówka airfield in Lwów due to engine failure.

The 7th FS' No. 10 fighter – series 253 Albatros D.III (Oef). The font of tactical numbers was modeled on the Austrian code pattern.

From T. Kopański collection

A series 253 D.III (Oef) repaired/rebuild at the Kraków Aircraft Facility, delivered to the 7th FS in late 1920.

Maj. Pil. Jerzy Kossowski, 253.266 to Pil. Maj. Aleksander Serednicki Chief of Staff of the Air Force Inspectorate, 253.233 to Rtm. Pil. Stanisław Jasiński Chief of Field Aviation, Polish Supreme Command. Other examples were used for training at flight schools. On May 3, 1919, flight instructor Sierż. Pil. Emil Majer was killed flying a D.III (Oef) belonging to the Basic Flight School in Kraków.

Overhauls of the type were carried out at the Warsztaty Szkoły Pilotów (Flight School Workshop) located at the Rakowice aerodrome, established on May 11, 1919, and later renamed the 2nd Aviation Repair Works. It commenced operations in autumn 1919 under engineer Por. Józef Krzemień, but unlike the name suggests the nature of the first assignments was in fact to rebuild aircraft. Minor repairs

Four series 253 Albatros D.III (Oef)s repaired at the Kraków Aircraft Facility, delivered to the 7th FS in late 1920.

were just a part of the daily work effort, its personnel was building complete airframe elements – wings, fuselages and empennages. Only metal structural components were used from the procured spare kits, but available wreckage was also cannibalized for spare parts. Such rebuilt planes took over numerical designations of their written off predecessors with 'K' prefix or 'A' affix, respectively after or before the serial number. It is estimated that the number of rebuilt Albatroses cost the equivalent of 20 brand new planes, not including funds spent on spare parts like the wings or empennage.

The Oeffag Albatros D.III was flown into combat by the 7th and 13th FSs.

The 7th 'Tadeusz Kościuszko' Fighter Squadron was a mixed American-Polish unit led by Maj. Pil. Cedric Faunt-Le-Roy that served the Commander-in-Chief as a back-up force. Its first assignment came on October 25, when at 12:50 Kpt. Pil. Corsi and Por.Pil. Idzikowski were ordered to intercept and force to land two German Gothas GL VII (both carried Ukrainian national insignia) spotted east of Stanisławów. The air patrol was uneventful as the pilots did not make contact with the enemy. Similar patrols were up in the following days but they also failed to come across any foreign planes. The unit's HQ in Lwów received important news – by order of Minister of Military Affairs Maj. Gen. Józef Leśniewski[66] dated December 31, 1919 "It is allowed for the 7th Fighter Squadron to be redesignated the 7th 'Tadeusz Kościuszko' Fighter Squadron (7 Eskadra Mysliwska im. Tadeusza Kościuszki)." The unit's emblem designed by Lt. Elliot Chess was also approved. Further changes were introduced in the air component – it was divided into two flights called 'Pulaski' and 'Kościuszko' led by Capt. Cooper (as his ancestor had known Kazimierz Pulaski) and Kpt. Pil. Corsi, respectively.

The first true combat sortie was flown on March 5, 1920, by Por. Pil. Harmon C. Rorison[67] (nicknamed Little Rory for his "5 ft 5" in boots"), who bombed and strafed Soviet forces at a small railroad station at Czudnowo. Over the target he encountered ground fire which damaged his fighter's fuellines. He nursed the plane to Płoskiwor where he landed, made a makeshift repair, and having taken off again after flying three and half hours he eventually landed at Tarnopol. During the upcoming months the 7th FS would undertake continued strike effort against the enemy.

The unit participated in an offensive against Kiev, where it flew primarily recce and attack sorties. It supported Polish troops in the fighting for and capturing of Berdyczów. Por. Pil. Noble was severely wounded in action.

Operating from Biała Cerkwia, the 7th was tasked to wreak havoc on Soviet river forces on the Dnestr River, destroying one steamer in the process. A flight of three, led by Capt. Cooper was stationed at the Kiev aerodrome from where it supported recce sorties of the 3rd and 16th Reconnaissance Squadrons (Eskadry Wywiadowcze).

In 1922, Kpt. Pil. Meriam Cooper[68] published his memoire in which he revived the fight against river steamboats on the Dnestr River.

"I was virtually last in a string of our planes approaching the Bolshevik fleet (each of us had its target predetermined by our Leader). Five Polish Bréguets and two Albatroses flown by Cpt. Corsi and Lt. Clark already commenced their attack. It was an extraordinary sight. I saw one of ours drop a bomb on an armored ship which immediately thereafter blew up. Within moments only debris was still floating on the surface of the river. Another battleship trying to dodge our bombs and machine gun fire sped headlong just to run aground to its doom. The rest of the fleet floated downstream at full steam while we pounded them with bombs and guns with great pleasure."

The Squadron carried out primarily attack missions but at the cost of losing Por. Pil. Rorison and Corsi.

From May 25, onwards when Capt. Crawford detected Budyonny's cavalry attacking Polish forces,

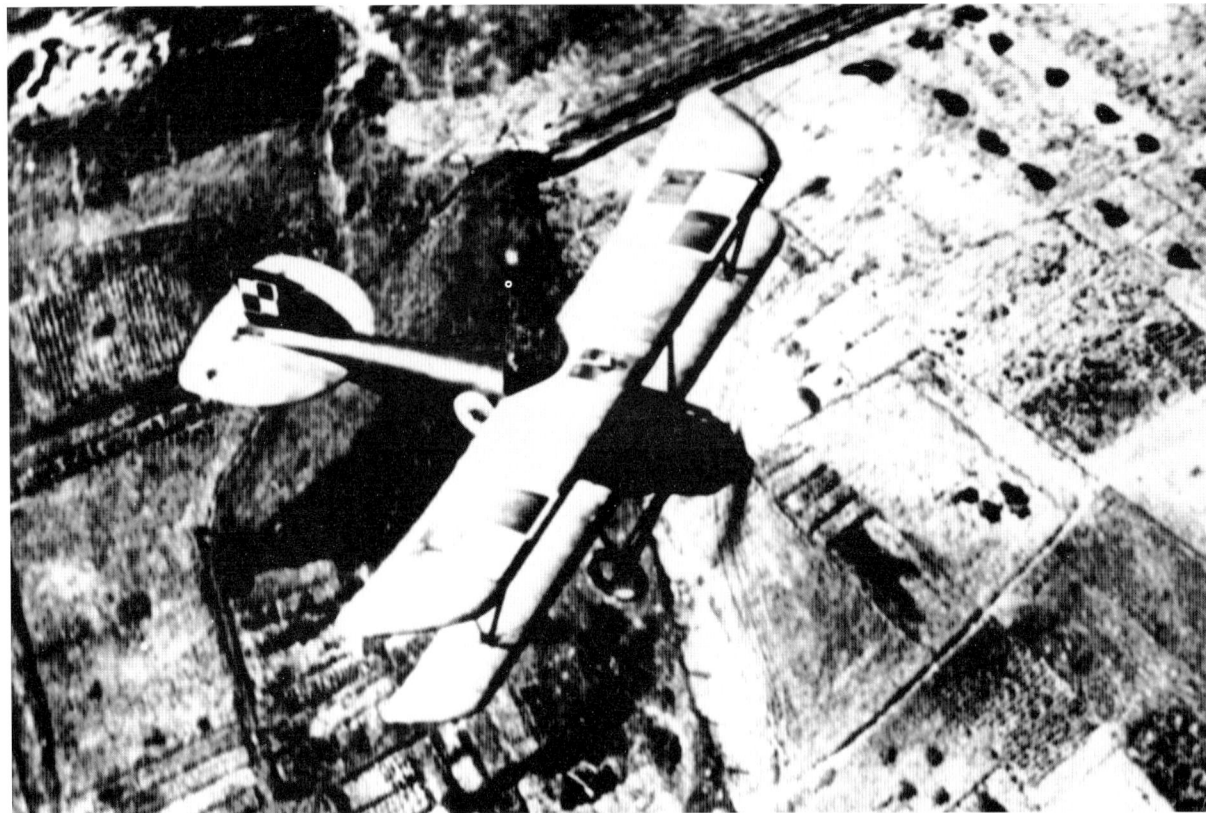

Albatros D.III in flight over Lwów. This plane was repaired at the Kraków Aircraft Facility and delivered to the 7th FS in late 1920.

the 7th FS was assigned mainly strike duties against the Cavalry Army. As the campaign progressed the unit withdrew towards Lwów. At Biała Cerkiew it was reinforced with Ansaldo Balillas and another group of U.S. volunteer pilots. The unit would operate both fighter types until the end of hostilities.

Being nominally a fighter unit, the 7th FS performed recce and attack sorties as it focused on harassing Soviet ground forces. Budyonny's 1st Cavalry Army in particular, suffering heavy losses in the process. On July 12, it mourned its greatest loss so far. That day Maj. Pil. Cooper (promoted to the rank of major) took off for a morning reconnaissance mission in the area of Brody, east of Lwów. When overflying the Styr River in search of Bolshevik forces he was hit by ground fire put up by the 1st Cavalry Army under Budionny's command. He crash-landed with a shot-up engine and was captured by the Cossacks. He escaped death from their hands as he wore a uniform without any rank insignia. Asked if he was an "officer master" he showed his toil worn hands covered in oil as each pilot took care of his aircraft's engine alone. After interrogation he was sent to a Moscow prison at the Alexander barracks. Cooper and three other Polish POWs held there escaped and having taken a long evasive route they reached Riga on October 1, 1920. In the meantime,

A series 253 Albatros D.III (Oef) from the 13th Fighter Squadron with pilot's personal insignia designed by Por. Pil. Patalas posing by his masterpiece.

Two photographs showing an Albatros D.II 910/16 from Jasta 5 that was flown by Lt. Max Böhme. Böhme was shot down by Lt. A.J. Pearson from No. 29 Sqdn. RFC on 4 March 1917. Three color Terrain Camouflage with pale blue lower wing surfaces and tailplane. The '8' digit was painted above and below fuselage in white and black.

three days after his doomed flight, the 7th FS lost three more aircraft[69].

On August 3, Por. Pil. Weber approached the airstrip at a far too great speed and crashed his D. III (Oef). The pilot was battered, with injured head and shoulder he was shortly hospitalized.

Two days later an Associated Press release reported:

"U.S. airmen from the 'Kosciuszko' Squadron tackle Budyonny's cavalry and infantry units in the Saret and Mikilecz sector. The number of losses inflicted on the enemy is estimated for 1600 killed with many other wounded." The news accurately reflected the volume of attack sorties the Squadron had flown.

One of its pilots was particularly unlucky. After returning from the hospital, Weber crashed another D.III (Oef) on August 3. The mishap was followed exactly a week later by Por. Pil. Konopka's unfortunate landing at the Zwiahl airstrip. He misjudged the distance to the ground and to avoid crashing into railroad rails he opened the throttle but failed to come clear of the open door of a dining car occupied by a cook who had been preparing supper. On

impact wings and the undercarriage fell apart but the fuselage slid inside. The pilot suffered a head wound and was rendered temporarily blind, but it was the unfortunate cook who took the brunt of the pilot's error. The impact lifted him off the floor and threw against a hot stove. He spent the following thirty minutes sitting in a water-filled tub. Fellow airmen got the pilot out of the plane, gave him first aid and drove him to a typhus hospital, where he was treated until the end of the month.

On August 11, the 7th FS returned to the Lewandówka aerodrome in Lwów to take part in defending the city against the advancing Budyonny's cavalry. The pilots were assigned to provide air support for offensive and defensive operations of Gen. Iwaszkiewicz's elements at the southern part of the front, hold the city and engage the Bolshevik cavalry. On August 16 alone the pilots flew 18 sorties attacking the advancing troops, supply columns, trains and vehicles in their area of responsibility. Buck Crawford was off the rooster as he was bed-ridden in the hospital Weber flew five missions, Corsi and Seńkowski four each. and Płk. Pil. Faunt-Le-Roy

A picture form the 13th FS' records showing two D.III (Oef)s. The second fighter sports a crested knight's helmet.

(by now promoted to colonel) three. The planes and crews were rushed into battle. In the meantime, the Polish ground forces launched a counter-offensive as the enemy had approached just 20 km of the city and had its church steeples in sight. Płk. Pil Faunt-Le-Roy who had been made 3rd Squadron's Leader in place for Kpt. Pil. Bastyr, ordered attack missions to be carried out by individual aircraft, with no bunching up on the ground queuing in line for fuel and to rearm. Planes were taking off every 15 minutes, gained altitude, bombed their targets from 700-800 m and strafed the enemy from low level until they ran out of ammunition. Lwów was saved without losing a single aircraft, but operations continued.

On September 23, the 7th FS received its final tasking of the war. It also received overhauled D.III (Oef)s. The new aircraft looked somehow different as they were painted green with the new framed checkerboard insignia and sported no tactical numbers. The 7th FS had flown 659 combat missions, logged 907 hours airborne, and lost 5 pilots.

In late 1920, the 2nd 'Wielkopolska' Aviation Squadron[70] (reconnaissance) was re-designated to 13 Fighter Squadron. In April the following year its name was again changed to the 13th FS. It was equipped with 11 D.III (Oef)s and based at Bobrujsko. No air opposition was encountered while the unit focused primarily on recce and attack missions. For bomb raids light bombs were taken aboard to be either dropped manually or using primitive bomb ejector racks the unit's mechanics had developed. A flight from the 13th FS was tasked to defend Minsk.

As the overwhelming Soviet forces advanced the FS fell back to Baranowicze, then to Hajnówka and Siedlce from where it was striking against enemy crossings over the Bug River.

In early August the 13th FS was redeployed to Siekierki near Warsaw to operate with Gen. Sikorski's 5th Army. In the course of the campaign the unit lost one pilot Sierż. Pil. Kazimierz Jankowski who had been shot down over Pułtusk. Several D.III (Oef)s were damaged by the Soviet anti-aircraft fire that had been growing more and more powerful.

In August 1920, the 13th FS was reinforced by Fokker D.VIIs and deployed to conduct attack runs in the area of Włocławek and Płock against Gaj-Chan's cavalry.

After capturing Białystok the 13th FS was transferred to an airstrip at Dojlidy where it was incorporated into the 2nd Army to operate in the Grodno-Lida sector. It was the last post of the unit before the armistice. By the end of the war the 2nd 'Wielkopolska' Squadron/13th FS had flown 547 combat sorties and logged 793 hours airborne. Four pilots were lost.

Por. Pil.. Patalas pictured next to one of his masterpieces – an insignia painted on Por. Pil. K. Jankowski's plane.

Fuselage wreckage of Por. Pil. Jankowski's Albatros D.III (Oef) on reaching the Kraków facility. Pilot's personal insignia and the unit's badge are clearly visible.

A fuselage of Por. Pil. Jankowski's rebuilt Albatros D.III ready for engine installation. The smaller, stabilizing fin fashioned after the original D.III design is clearly visible.

A repaired Por. Pil. Jankowski's Albatros D.III (Oef) cleared for assignment to a line unit. The powerplant is fully embedded in the fuselage.

The Oeffag D.III remained in service until 1923. The last examples to be withdrawn belonged to the Advanced Flight School (AFS) in Grudziądz. On August 30, 1922, inventory rosters of squadrons of the 1st and 3rd Aviation Regiment (3 Pułk Lotniczy) and the AFS totaled 11 airworthy D.IIIs. The 2nd Aviation Regiment (2 Pułk Lotniczy) had 14 still flyable and 9 planned for scrapping. That was 34 altogether (while only 38 Albatros D.III (Oef)s had been procured).

Colors and Markings

For the German air service, its recognition emblem was a black cross called "Patée" of fixed proportions and height, initially usually painted on a white square. It was introduced on both sides of the rudder, upper and lower[71] wing surfaces and on either side of the fuselage. Sometimes it also appeared on

Albatros D.III (Oef) 253.237 undergoing another overhaul. Note its unusual serial format: D.III.237.

the elevator. Later the white square was replaced with thin white outline around the cross to reduce its visibility. Its shape was changed in 1917 to a straight Balkan cross.

Throughout its service the Albatros carried the following paint schemes:

• a plain (natural) camouflage scheme: clear-doped natural linen and clear-varnished plywood (varnished plywood produces a warm straw yellow color) with metal (aluminum) panels and spinner. The metal parts were also covered with a greenish-grey or plain green protective varnish. The wooden fuselage was often stained and lacquered, which made the aircraft's fuselage look dark brown,

• a two color Terrain Camouflage scheme (on all Albatros D.Is from production batch D.421-D.435): the upper wing surfaces and tailplane in large patches of olive green and rust brown[72]. The lower surfaces, undercarriage and hubcaps were pale sky blue. The rudder either retained its natural canvas skin color or was painted using one of the camouflage patterns. Metal cowling parts, acces panels covers, the propeller hub and struts were greenish light grey. Some aircraft had the fuselage sprayed in irregular patches on the tops and sides in the olive and rust brown colors, with the bottom of the fuselage painted in pale sky blue (for example Albatros D.II 435/16),

• a three color[73] Terrain Camouflage scheme: the upper surfaces of wings and tailplane in patches of dark olive green[74], rust brown[75] and pale green[76] which divided the surfaces into three, five or six sections. Seven different paint schemes were used

on various Albatros D.Is and D.IIs. For example on Albatros D.II from production batch D.472-D.501 the upper wing surfaces were painted in six near equal areas with the following colors applied diagonally starting from the left wingtip): rusty brown, pale green, olive dark green, rusty brown, pale green, olive dark green. The rudder and elevator followed the pattern with three color sections (pale green, rusty brown, dark olive green). The rudder was usually painted the same color as the middle stripe on the tailplane, i.e. in rusty brown. Various manufacturers used different shade schemes, on the LVG-built D.II (LVG) and O.A.W. examples in particular. Remaining elements of the airframe were varnished using the plain camouflage or in a three-color pattern (for production batch D.890-D.939). The tri-color Terrain camouflage was also used on the D.III and D.V. Bottom surfaces were painted sky light blue,

• on April 12, 1917 Ideflieg ordered that the rusty brown color must be replaced with purple[77] (mauve). The requirement originated from the fact that in combat the Albatros was frequently mistaken for French aircraft as the opposition used green and chestnut. Generally multi color Camouflage scheme was used on upper surfaces. The lower canvas-skinned surfaces either retained their natural finish or were pale sky blue. Aluminum sheets were all painted green or gray,

• another pattern had the fuselage in plain finish with tiny green spots giving a mottled effect, upper wing surfaces and the tailplane in one of the multi color Camouflage schemes with sky pale blue undersurfaces. Aluminum sheets were all painted green or gray (sometimes on grey panels green stapple was applied) (for example Albatros D.III 2243/16, or D.Va 5815/18),

• on some silver white Albatroses a dark green dapple camouflage on sides and upper surfaces was sometimes applied. Such an example was flown in autumn 1917 by Oblt. Heinrich Gontermann from Jasta 17.

In 1917 a new pattern lozenge fabric[78] (mosaic) skin canvas was introduced. It comprised of irregular- or regular-shaped pentagons and hexagons arranged in either four- or five-color patterns. The polygons were of various colors, shapes and dimensions.

Each of the camouflage schemes featured a unique color pallette with darker shades on the upper surfaces and lighter on the bottom.

The OAW plant occasionally glued the mosaic canvas onto plywood-skinned sections, but a hand-painted pattern similar to the hexagon scheme could be seen on plywood fuselages as well.

It was also a common practice to leave the fuselage in its natural finish and cover the upper wing surface with one of the modular patterns or apply the lozenge fabric. Metal parts and the fairing covering the undercarriage axle were usually painted dark green or gray.

The Albatros W4s serving in the naval aviation were:
• in plain finish,
• painted all grey blue,
• on 3 April 1917 the SVK (See-Flugzeug Versuchs Kommando) advised the manufacturers of the new finishing requirements. The order stated that "all surfaces visible from above (wings, the fuselage, floats and tailplane) were to be painted in hexagons 30 cm across in three colors: grey-blue, grey-violet and grey-brown. All the surfaces visible from the side would be grey-blue (fuselage, rudder, floats and all struts) while all surfaces as viewed from below were to be painted light grey (fuselage, floats). The under surfaces of wings and tailplane were to retain their natural linen color",

• as of April 1918 all surfaces visible from above (wings, the fuselage, floats and tailplane) were to be covered with a new printed fabric with irregular hexagons in three colors: blue grey, grey-violet and grey-brown. The irregular hexagons were 155x200 mm and skewed 5 degrees on the width of the fabric. Other parts of the airframe were painted as noted above.

On both sides of the fuselage a large black Marine (Navy) aircraft number was painted.

After the end of hostilities the Albatros D.IIs, D.IIIs, D.Vs and D.Vas belonging to Zentrale Abnahme Kommision[79], ZAK for short, were painted all white.

Apart from camouflage schemes, each plane wore black or white manufacturer's serial on the vertical stabilizer or on both sides of the fuselage behind the cockpit. There was also weight data, operating descriptions, arrows marking suitable hold points and alignment lines for wing and tailplane angle wedges. The serial followed by description also marked all major aircraft components.

Colors of airframe elements usually constituted unit colors (see Appendix IV) as well. For instance the tailplane was striped, in geometric patterns or painted in the unit's characteristic color. Occasionally emblems were also applied.

The color of an aircraft or its airframe elements was at the same time pilot's personal emblem. Apart from a unique color, initials, inscriptions and alle-

Albatros D.III (Oef) 253.217 is believed to have been overhauled as its unusual fuselage modex is based on the German Alb.D.III 27/19. The wings and tailplane are covered with Austrian spiral-pattern canvas.

Plt. Lt. Doroszewski crashed an Albatros D.III (Oef) fitted with additional lower wings strengthening support taken after the Germans. It was camouflaged either in natural colors or light grey. Note Teves und Braun radiator installed on this plane and unusual form of aircraft number ALB. D.III 216 painted on the rudder.

Another crashed D.III (Oef), this one at the Radom airfield. The example featured an interesting pilot's insignia on the fuselage 'RE...?' plus a dead woman's head with hair.

An Albatros D.II ex 53.06 overhauled in Czechoslovakia This aircraft belonged to FALCO company and was piloted by Zdeněk Lhota.

gorical emblems could be seen on individual fighters as well. The red Albators D.III of the Red Baron Manfred von Richthofen is the best known example, but Carl Allmenröder flew a red Albatros too. There were also black fighters of Lt. Ernst Udet, Josef Jacobs, Otto Kissenberth, Edward Ritter von Schleich and Herman Goering. A whole book could be written on the colors of German aces, but even that would not have covered the topic in all detail as not all records of color schemes used during the Great War survived in photographs or descriptions.

Some of the German fighters captured by the French, British or Australians retained their original paint schemes, Allied national insignia being the only addition, while others were repainted in the new owners' standard paint schemes.

The Albatros D.II(Oef) and D.III(Oef) were painted differently in the **Austro-Hungarian air service**.

The k.u.k Luftfahrtruppen recognition marking was introduced in 1913. At first it was Austrian national colors, i.e. red, white and red or red and white stripes, painted on the fuselage, wing, vertical fin and the tailplane. With the outbreak of WW1 Austria received from Germany large quantities of military hardware wearing German markings. Soon the land-based air service inherited the black 'Patee' cross that would be painted on the top and bottom wing surfaces, both sides of the rudder and occasionally on both sides of the fuselage; initially

directly on the skin fabric, but later on, following the German pattern, on the white or gray undercoat. There was also a version with a thin white rim. The 'Patee' had the following dimensions:[80] H = 0.5, 0.7, 1.0 and 1.4 m.

In 1918 again following the German practice, Austro-Hungary introduced the Balkan cross featuring straight arms and a thin white rim. The marking was even applied to undercarriage wheel hubs on some examples, though the general principle was to paint it on the fixed elements of the wings and the rudder.

After the end of the Great War the D.II (Oef)s used in the Carinthia campaign had vertical red-white-red stripes on the rudder.

The aircraft that rolled out of the Oeffag plant received the following paint schemes:

The plain (natural) finish was the usual standard, especially on the 53 and 153 series: clear-doped natural or whitened linen, clear-varnished plywood (varnished plywood produces warm straw yellow) with metal (aluminum) panels and spinner.

In 1918, aircraft manufacturers including Oeffag began to apply camouflage using a number of pattern-covered canvas types (we describe only those used on the Albatros (Oef)).

Records reveal that one Albatros D. III(Oef) serial 153.112 received hand-made pattern-covered canvas skin resembling the German scheme. Its colors remain unknown.

An Albatros D.III, serial unknown, seen here at a factory airstrip.

A printed spiral pattern fabric of three colors: greyish yellow, light brown and deep green produced by J Backhausen and Sohne of Vienna (pattern varnished on a 75 x 75 cm square cotton canvas 170 cm wide). Occasionally the canvas was used as skin for plywood structure elements. The pattern was applied on the fourth batch of 153 series Albatroses and series 253 aircraft manufactured between July and September 1918. The under wing and tailplane surfaces retained the natural finish of clear-doped linen. Some series 253 Albatros D.III (Oef)s featured light grey blue bottom wing surfaces.

Experience gained on the Italian Front led to introduction of camouflage schemes. Fighters assigned to Fliegeretapppenpark and other units as well sported an array of camouflage patterns. Top wing, tailplane and fuselage surfaces were covered with 2-4 cm dots made using a sponge with green paint. They neither had sharp edges nor were of identical shade. As they were closely arranged, they appeared from a distance to be all green or olive.

Other patterns comprised of carefully painted, regularly arranged dots in various colors:
- dark green, grayish green, grayish yellow,
- deep green, dark green,
- dark green, grayish yellow,
- dark green, grayish green, green, olive yellow, olive.

There were also variations of these patterns, e.g. closely speckled, sometimes overlapping dots. Each dot was painted using a sponge or ragged swab. The bottom surfaces of wings and the tailplane retained their natural linen finish, only occasionally painted blue.

Aircraft left in their natural colors had their top wing, tailplane and fuselage surfaces painted with green undercoat and then beige or light yellowish green spirals, up to 10 cm I diameter. Hpt. Godwin Brumowski flew one of those (Albatros (Oef) D.III 53.27) in Flik 41J, although his first aircraft to wear this particular paint scheme was Phonix-built D. 28.69. The pattern was applied on other (Oef)s in the Flik, as well as in Fliks 46F and 35D who attempted to copy it.

Some series 153 (Oef)s in Flik 2D had large olive-brown and dark blue dots.

Top wing, tailplane, fuselage, vertical fin surfaces as well as wheel hubs were green covered with hand-painted yellowish brown (mustard shade) spirals atop. The pattern was used for Flik41/J and those Fliks that received Albatros (Oef)s from the same Fliegeretappenpark[81].

All-brown aircraft, including bottom surfaces, e.g. those of Flik 61/J,

Top and lateral surfaces had greenish blue dots, while bottoms were blue – the pattern was mainly used by Flik 55/J.

The Albatros W.4s delivered from Germany probably retained the colors that had been applied according to the orders from April 1917 and 1918. Perhaps after receiving the type the Austro-Hungarian naval aviation service added its characteristic recognition marks (red-white-red stripes with an emblem on the white stripe) on the rudder and naval serial numbers on the fuselage.

It was required that each aircraft carried its type and series numbers comprised of 0.25 m black numerals, on each side of the fuselage (as shown in the picture). Individual airframe components had their serials marked with much smaller lettering – 0.15 m – in different font. The Albatros (Oef) logo was on the fuselage nose section under the engine. Underneath there was the aircraft type, engine and weight reference data.

Unit emblems were seldom painted as each unit was recognized by the font and color of its tactical number. For instance, Flik 55J had a white numeral shaded in black, with characteristic black wheel hubs, nose fuselage section and struts. Flik 24 was recognized for its D.II (Oef) and D.III (Oef) with black noses, struts and wheel hubs. Flik 61J had various color stripes on the top wing, fuselage and empennage surfaces. Pilots often painted their personal emblems mainly on the fuselage. All pilots of Flik 3/J had their personal emblems. Aircraft flown by Solski, Tomicki and Stec – Albatros D.III 153.173 and 253.08 – had the checkerboard marking. Available photos of the 253.08 show that on the starboard the upper right and lower left squares were red, while the port side[82] featured inverted colors. Although emblems on either side of the fuselage were mirrored they could differ as proved by the Albatros D.III (Oef) 153.167 from Flik 2D and 153.169 from Flik 42J.

An interesting pattern evolved among pilots who began to use a number of personal emblems to identify them in the air. For example Godwin Brumowski had 4 different emblems, not to mention his all-red aircraft. Other pilots like Frank Linke Crawford also had four, Friedrich Navratil and Stefan Stec just two.

Polish Albatros Colors

The Polish Albatroses flew either painted in one of the German patterns or using its variation developed by the Poznań-based aircraft shop at Ławnica or a pattern from the Central Aviation Workshop in Warsaw. The most frequent solution was an all-green fuselage, green and purple segment pattern (copy of the German design) on the top wing and tailplane surfaces, with light blue bottom surfaces. A small number of fighters received mosaic canvas skin for the wings and empennage.

The Polish recognitions marks were painted on the top upper wing surfaces, the bottom lower wing surfaces, either side of the rudder and only occasionally on the fuselage between the cockpit and tailplane. The aircraft that served in Wielkopolska units received additional white and red stripes on the nose section of the fuselage (on the propeller spinner and the cowls) as well as stripes and chevrons on the fuselage between the cockpit and empennage, although sometimes the chevrons were also painted on the top surfaces of both wings. Some examples repaired at Ławica received their numbers and white rectangles containing the aircraft reference data on both sides of the fuselage. The Ławica-based Flight School planes had black or white (silver) numbers on light or green fuselages, respectively. The D.IIIs that were repaired at the CAW (e.g. 0.01 and 0.11) were all-grey.

The Polish D.III (Oef)s retained the colors applied by the Oeffag plant, i.e. their natural finish. A number of planes received spiral pattern fabric on the wings and tailplane. Soon as repairs were carried out new mosaic patterns appeared. The most popular was: green fuselage, top surfaces of wings and the tailplane also green or their canvas left unpainted with bottom surfaces light blue or unpainted as well.

An Albatros D.III (Oef) from the 7th FS takes off at Lwów in November 1919.

Por. Pil. Rorison by his No. 3 Albatros D.III (Oef) featuring the emblem of the 7th FS.

That scheme was characteristic for the Kraków repair plant.

Some Albatros D.III (Oef)s received the German mosaic or Austrian spiral-patterned canvas skin for the wings and tailplane.

The Polish recognition marking was applied on the top upper wing surface, bottom lower wing surface, both sides of the rudder and seldom on the fuselage behind the cockpit and the empennage. There is, however, something intriguing about the marking painted on the majority of the acquired D.III (Oef)s: they featured the frame-less checkerboard pattern though by the time of their delivery to Poland the new framed checkerboard had been introduced. Questions have been raised if perhaps the Oeffag plant received the initial drawings of the marking without the frame. As the aircraft's service life progressed, especially after each repair carried out at Kraków, the planes got the framed marking. Other elements sometimes painted on selected (Oef)s included the example number with type reference data according to the 'Wielkopolska' unit style or to the CAW pattern with '0' representing the aircraft type and the registration number after a dot. For instance, the 0.20 – the crashed plane depicted here. The Kraków repair plant had a standard practice of adding the 'K' prefix to the original manufacturer's serials.

The Squadron emblems were painted on all Albatros D.III (Oef)s in the 7th 'Tadeusz Kościuszko' Fighter Squadron and the 13th FS. Furthermore, the 7th introduced nose color markings to represent individual flights: red for the Kościuszko flight, blue for the Pulaski. Dimensions and shape of the colored area differed. In the course of war the red noses were repainted as the Polish infantry and cavalry opened up on such aircraft mistakenly taking them for Soviet machines.

Personal pilot emblems were painted most often on the (Oef)s in the 13th FS. Nearly all fighters[83] had emblems designed by Por. Pil. Patalas. His motives varied largely, e.g. Por. Pil. Jankowski had a skull, but there was also an angel's head with wings, a knight's helmet with a crest, Leda playing with Zeus transformed into a swan, or an attacking eagle. A wide variety of other personal emblems appeared on the Albatros D.III (Oef)s, e.g. a skull with female hair and a "RE…" inscription[84] or Sierż. Pil Emil Mayer's arrow-pierced heart. After his death on May 5, 1919, in a plane crash someone added his name and the date of the crash.

After the end of hostilities personal emblems were used by the 7th FS and the Advanced Flight School.

APPENDICES

APPENDIX I AUSTRO-HUNGARIAN RANKS

Rank name	Abbreviations	Name in English
Zugsführer	Zugsf.	Lance Corporal
Korporal	Korp.	Corporal, an enlisted rank.
Feldwebel	Feldw.	Sergeant
Stabsfeldwebel	Stabsfeldw.	Staff Setgeant, noncommissioned officer rank.
Fähnrich	Fhr.	Ensign
Stellvertreter	Stv.	Warrant
Offiziersstellvertreter	Offstv.	Acting officer, highest noncommissioned officer rank.
Leutnant	Lt.	Secound lieutnant
Leutnant in der Reserve	Lt. d. R.	Reserve Secound lieutnant
Linienschiffsleutnant		Lieutenant Commander rank in K.u.K Navy.
Oberleutnant	Oblt.	First Lieutenant
Oberleutnant in der Reserve	Oblt. d. R.	Reserve First Lieutenant
Rittmeister	Rittm.	A cavalry Captain
Hauptman	Hptm.	Captain
Oberst:		Colonel.

Beobachteroffizier (BO): Observation officer.
Feldpilot (FP): Field Pilot, a title awarded after approximately ten combat missions This was added before rank name, for example FP. Hpt
Stabsoffizier der Luftfahrtruppen (Stoluft): Staff officer of the aviation troops assigned to an army.

APPENDIX II GERMAN RANKS

Rank name	Abbreviation	Name in English
Flieger/Schütze		Private
Gefreiter	Gefr.	Lance Corporal
Obergefreiter	Obgefr.	Lance Corporal major
Unteroffizier	Uffz.	Corporal
Feldwebel	Fw.	Sergeant
Vizefeldwebel	Vfw.	Sergeant major
Offizerstellvertreter	Offstv.	Warrant officer
Leutnant	Lt.	Secound lieutnant
Leutnant der Reserve	Lt. d. R.	Reserve 2 lieutnant
Oberleutnant	Oblt.	Lieutenant
Oberleutnant der Reserve	Oblt. d. R.	Reserve lieutnant
Hauptman	Hptm.	Captain
Rittmeister	Rittm.	Cavalry captain
Major	Mjr.	Major

APPENDIX III POLISH RANKS

Rank name	Abbreviation	Name in English
Kapral	Kpr.	Corporal
Plutonowy	Plut.	Lance Corporal
Sierżant	Sierż.	Sergeant
Starszy Sierżant	St. Sierż	Sergeant First Class
Sierżant sztabowy	Sierż. Szt..	Staff Setgeant
Chorąży	Chor.	Ensign
Podporucznik	Ppor.	Secound lieutnant
Porucznik	Por.	Lieutenant
Kapitan	Kpt.	Captain
Rotmistrz	Rtm.	Cavalry Capitan
Major	Mjr.	Major
Podpułkownik	Ppłk.	Lieutenant Colonel
Pułkownik	Płk.	Colonel

APPENDIX IV
EXAMPLES OF ALBATROS JAGDSTAFFEL MARKINGS

Jasta 2	white tail, black band round fuselage aft of the spinner or only black spinner
Jasta 4	black spiral band around fuselage
Jasta 5	green tail outlined with red, red spinners
Jasta 6	black and white zebra striping on rear fuselage and tail and bottom wing surface at the wing root; black extremes of the lower wing (up to the last rib); white extremes of the fuselage (without the vertical fin on some aircraft)
Jasta 10	yellow nose and cowling band with small black numbers on the fuselage front
Jasta 11	red front section of the fuselage, undercarriage wheel hubs, pyramid and wing struts
Jasta 12	black aft section of the fuselage and the tailplane
Jasta 13	green front section of the fuselage up to the second pyramid coupling; the rest of the fuselage and the tailplane dark blue Another scheme applied when a unit was transitioning to the Fokker Dr.I featured a white aft section of the fuselage, tailplane and spinner
Jasta 14	horizontal black and white band on the fuselage
Jasta 15	red front section of the fuselage up to the second pyramid coupling; the rest of the fuselage and the tailplane blue
Jasta 16B	black aft section of the fuselage, tailplane and spinner
Jasta 17	on Albatros D.II white-black-white-black-white bands aft fuselage national insignia dark (black or red) aft section of the fuselage and the tailplane
Jasta 18	red front section of the fuselage up to the second pyramid coupling; the rest of the fuselage and the tailplane dark blue
Jasta 19	black and yellow stripes on the fuselage, two vertical stripes between the cockpit and the tailplane
Jasta 23B	white stripe on the aft section of the fuselage and the tailplane, black aft section of the fuselage and tailplane
Jasta 25	white fin and fuselage part aft tailplane, black or red rudders and band in front of fuselage
Jasta 27	black fuselage, tail unit and wheel covers. H. Goering's aircraft had white tail unit and aircraft nose rest of fuselage was black
Jasta 28W	yellow tailplane and rudder with two black stripes parallel to the centerline
Jasta 32B	a black aft section of the fuselage; a white front section of the fuselage and spinner
Jasta 34B	silver-white fuselages
Jasta 35B	white chevron on the upper wing
Jasta 37	tail surfaces were painted in diagonal black/white stripes, black spinner
Jasta 50	light blue and red diagonal stripes on the tailplane and rudder
Jasta 57	light blue vertical tail unit and fuselage from the cockpit aft
Jasta 71	4 white and 3 black stripes on tail (dividing the tail into 7 equal parts), white spinner
Jasta 76B	white and blue (sometimes just white) front section of the fuselage
MFJ 1 (Marine Feld Jagdstaffel)	yellow nose with cowling band and rudder and tailplane
Kampfeinsitzer Staffel 8W ('Kest' – a Home Defense Squadron)	light colored (reportedly silver grey front and aft sections of the fuselage and the tailplane)

Albatros Basic Technical Specification

Aircraft Specification and Performance / Albatros Variant	D.I	D.II	D.II (LVG)	D.II (Oef)	D.III	D.III (OAW)	D.III (Oef) 53	D.III (Oef) 153	D.III (Oef) 253	D.IV	D.V	D.Va	D.Va (OAW)	W.4 serial 911	D.VII	Dr.I
Engine output [KW]	111/118	118	118	136	118/129	118	136	148	168	118	118/129	129	129	118	144	118
Upper wing span [m]	8.5	8.5	8.5	8.5	9.05	9.05	9	9	9	9.05	9.05	9.05	9.05	9.5	9.32	8.7
Lower wing span [m]	8	8	8.1	8	8.81	8.81	8.7	8.7	8.70	-	8.73	8.73	8.73	9.2	-	-
Length [m]	7.4	7.4	7.4	7.35	7.33	7.33	7.35	7.35	7.35	7.33	7.33	7.33	7.33	8.5	6.62	7.3
Height [m]	2.64	2.95	2.95	2.71	2.98	2.98	2.8	2.8	2.8	-	2.7	2.7	2.7	3.65	2.68	2.42
Lifting surface [m^2]	24.5	24.9	25.2	24	20.9	20.9	20.64	20.64	20.64	-	21.24	21.24	21.24	31.6	-	-
Bulk weight [kg]	694	673	710	648	673 (735)	603.5	690	709	716	-	620	687	730.5	790	630	-
Gross take-off weight [kg]	921.5	898	937.5	898	906 (1060)	891	942	961	1005	-	852	937	950.5	1070	885	-
Max. speed [km/h]	175	175	165	170	165/175	165	174	188	202	165	165/187	170	170	160	204	-
Climb-rate to 1000 m [min]	6	5	-	4'30	2'30	-	2'30	2'30	2'15	-	4'20	4	-	5	7*	-
to 3000m [min]	15'40	12'40	-	-	11'10	-	11'1	10'15	9'15	-	14.50	-	-	11'30	-	-
to 5000m [min]	40	37	-	-	24.30	-	24.3	21'40	20'15	32	35	-	-	-	-	-
Ceiling [m]	5200	5200	5200	approx. 5000	5800	5800	approx. 5000	approx. 5000	approx. 5000	-	5700	6250	6250	3000	-	-
Flight endurance [h]	1.5	1.5	1.5	-	2	2	-	-	-	-	2	2	2	3	2	-

Brackets reveal weight of examples with structural strength improvements
*time of climbing to 2000m
Various sources provided various weight data for the same aircraft variant.

Bibliography

Peter L. Grey & Ian R. Stair, *Albatros fighters of World War 1*, Wingspan Publications, Oxford 1979.

Peter Gray & Owen Thetford, *German Aircraft of the First World War*, Doubleday&Company, Inc. Garden City, New York 1962.

Zych Płodowski, *O budowie płatowców*, Warszawa 1925

Peter L. Grey,*The Albatros D.III*, Profile Publications Ltd. Windsor, Berkshire 1965

Peter L. Grey, *The Albatros D.V*, Profile Publications Ltd. Windsor Berkshire, England 1965

John F. Connors, *Albatros fighters in action*, Squadron/Signal publications Carrollton 1996

Alex Imrie, *Pictorial History of the German Army Air service 1914-1918*, Henry Regnery Company-Chicago 1971

Alex Imrie, *German Fighter Units 1914-may 1917*, Osprey Publishing Company Oxford 1978

Alex Imrie, *German Fighter Units June 1917-1918*, Osprey Publishing Company Oxford 1978

Norman Franks, *Albatros Aces of World War 1*, Osprey Publishing Company Oxford-New York 2000

Greg Van Wyngarden, *Albatros Aces of World War 1 Part 2*, Osaprey Publishing Company Oxford-New York 2007

Greg Van Wyngarden, *Jagdstaffel 2 „Boelcke"*, Osprey Publishing Company Oxford-New York 2007

Greg Van Wyngarden, *„Richthofen's Circus"*, Osprey Publishing Company Oxford-New York 2004

Greg Van Wyngarden, *Jagdgeschwader Nr II*, Osprey Publishing Company Oxford-New York 2005

Christopher Chant, *Austro-Hungarian Aces of World War 1*, Osprey Publishing Company, Oxford-New York 2001.

Terry C. Treadwell & Allan C. Wood, *German Fighter Aces of World War One*, Tempus Publishing Ltd. Stroud Gloucestershire 2003

P.M. Grosz, *Albatros D.III(Oef) Windsock Datafile 19 Albatros Productions LTD* , Berkhamsted Hertfordshire 1990

Martin O'Connor, *Austro-Hungarian Air Aces*, Falcon Field Mesa Arizona 1986.

Tomasz Goworek, *Pierwsze samoloty myśliwskie lotnictwa polskiego, Sigma Not*, Warszawa 1991.

Vaclav Nemecek, *Vojenska letadla 1, Nase Vojsko*, Praha 1974

Magazines: *Wings, Airpower, Air Classics, Air Enthusiast Quarterly, Modelarz, Skrzydlata Polska, Scale Models, Letectvi+Kosmonautika.*

Endnotes

[1] Meissner, J., Jak dziś Pamiętam (I vividly remember), Iskry, Warszawa, 1971

[2] More on the Nieuport can be found in the Nieuport 1-27 from Famous Airplanes series published by Kagero

[3] Eng. Robert Thelen was an aviation pioneer and director of Deutsche Wright Gesellschaft. From Apr. 1, 1912 he headed the design bureau, in the summer 1914 he was appointed the technical director for Albatros Flugzeugwerke G.m.b.H.

[4] Designation introduced by the Albatros works after the cease of hostilities

[5] Losing the lower wing meant losing steering in the upper wing ailerons as their steering cables went through the lower wing,

[6] The static tests conducted on the wings in January 1917 proved that the spar is too far away from the leading edge.

[7] Similar solutions were applied by the French on their Nieuports and Spads VII and XIII, though the cameras were mounted in the fuselage.

[8] This and three other planes participated in a competition for a fighter aircraft, held on January 21-28, 1918. The Albatros scored behind the top-scoring planes.

[9] See Fokker D.VII described in Famous Airplanes series published by Kagero in 2004

[10] Lesson learnt from Fokker Dr.I deficiency, which tended to lose this aileron-equipped wing.

[11] With the prototypes and the test batch with serials 747, 785-786, 902-911, the total of produced Albatros W.4s is 118 examples.

[12] Imperial and Royal Royal Air Corps

[13] By Austrian we do not necessarily mean pure Austrian nationals, but subjects of the multinational monarchy.

[14] The Phönix works was also considered for manufacturing the Albatros, but the idea was abandoned as the plant had been working on a fighter of their own.

[15] That was the original designation of license-built Albatros planes manufactured at Oeffag.

[16] The aircraft manufactured in Austria had a numerical designation: for instance, number 5 stood for Oeffag, and number 3 denoted aircraft type; following the dot was the number of an example. If the structure was redesigned, a series – Bauart number was added before the manufacturer's number. Thus designation Albatros (Oef) D.III 153.27 belonged to the twenty seventh example of Albatros manufactured by Oeffag under series 2.

[17] After manufacturing 290 examples.

[18] In practice, the spinner was often removed to improve cooling. Another reason was its propensity to fly off in flight, which inevitably led to airframe damage.

[19] Like the French Nieuports, the Albatros aircraft lost wings in dive due to their twisting caused by single spars in lower wings.

[20] A Fliegerkompanie was equipped with 6-8 aeroplanes.

[21] It is interesting that the Austrians never acquired the German synchronization system.

[22] Ordnance Test Squadron.

[23] It served with Flik 68 and after the crash it was rebuilt as a photo-recce version.

[24] Some 286 series 153 fighters had been built according to Air Enthusiast Quarterly One.

[25] For instance, the 253.116 and 253.118 were fitted with the older wing variant, while the 253.81 and 253.108 received the new strengthened wing.

[26] The Albatros D.III (Oef)s were designed with aircraft-to-aircraft interchangeable airframe elements, e.g. wings.

[27] Flik is an abbreviation of Flieger kompagne-flying company, a military unit equivalent to a squadron.

[28] It had further effect on the Polish Air Force.

[29] There were five FLARS' numbered I through V and one without a numerical code in Berlin collecting aircraft manufactured in Germany.

[30] Rear-area aviation park supplying equipment and fighting materials to selected front sectors

31 The highest known number is 253.260.

32 The rate of fire was improved by a refinement developed by Ludwik Kral. The upgraded Schwarzlose fired 600-630 rounds per minute.

33 Army Flight Depot, an organization unit responsible for maintaining and overhauling planes.

34 After Max Immelman, he was the second pilot to be awarded that distinction.

35 Its flight crew was: Cpt. Paul du Peuty and Sus-Lt. De Boutiny.

36 Noteworthy is the two-month delay period between the acceptance of the Albatros D.I and the delivery of the first example to a combat unit.

37 The aircraft was the D.II from the first pre-production batch of 12 examples. P.M. Grosz claimed D.388/16 was the D.III prototype. It may be concluded that the D.I, D.II and D.III were designed at the same time without any interim 'development stage' designs. The D.III underwent strength tests in September 1916.

38 At that time Jasta 6's was equipped with 6 planes.

39 Some sources claim it was a DH2.

40 This unit did receive a single Albatros in 1916.

41 A.E. Ferko hypothesizes that Richthofen could have been hit by a round fired by another Albatros as accurate fire from 300 m was impossible.

42 Flown by Ltn. Niederdorf and Brauneck.

43 Most pilots honed their skill by flying two-seaters, hence their perfect awareness of their weak points.

44 'B' marked a Bavarian Jasta, 'W' a Wurtenberg, and 'S' a Saxxon. No letter affix marked a Prussian unit. Only servicemen from a given German Empire constituent duchy could serve in their 'home' units.

45 Hence JG II was called Geschwader "Berthold".

46 Fighter units were designatod with 'J' for Jagd added after Flik's numerical code. Hence Flik 41J meant a fighter squadron.

47 He trained with Jasta 24 on the French front where he flew an Albatros D.II serial D.1769/16. He knew the 'Red Baron' Manfred von Richthofen who most probably inspired him to paint his Albatros red.

48 An interesting character who flew with a white and red checker pattern on his Hansa Brandenburg D.I 28.17. The pattern was also painted on Linke-Crawford's 28.40. Karl Meindl and Walter Schroeder in his book Brandenburg D.I note that Linke's chessboard was black and white.

49 Killed with his observer Por. Obs. Motylewski during fighting with the Ukrainians.

50 When taking over Flik 3J, Navratil had claimed one air victory he had won in Flik 41J.

51 S.Stec reached Flik 3/J in March 1918.

52 Reserve Lieutenant.

53 On August 10, 1918, Stec flying an Albatros D.III(Oef) 253.08 shot down an enemy plane over Monte Passubio.

54 He died in Flik 41J's D.III(Oef) 153.54 on November 6, 1917, killed by Cpt. Francesco Baracca and Tenente. Giuliamo Parvis.

55 Tadeusz Malinowski

56 Probably Otto Forster

57 Staff Sergeant.

58 A report by Repair Aviation Company.

59 After "Ku Czci Poległych Lotników - Book of Fallen Airmen."

60 A Polish manual "Płatowiec pościgowy typu Albatros D-III" published by Technical Department of Ministry of Military Affairsin 1919 (second supplemented edition).

61 Air Obeserver School later renamed to the Officer Air Observer School.

62 T. Gaworek lists 17 examples.

63 Unlike in Germany, in Poland they were popularly referred to as Oeffag D.III – Order No. 29, technical revision of March 15, 1920.

64 Serials 212, 218, 219, 220, 222, 229, 234 and 235.

65 Serials 213, 221, 223, 230, 232

66 Officer Order No. 5 of Dec. 31, 1919, ref. no. CA W IWL archive vol. 2.

67 When flying in the 22th Aero Squadron he destroyed 3 Fokker D.VIIs.

68 Kpt. Meriam Cooper, *Meriam Cooper Faunt-Le-Roy i jego Eskadra w Polsce*, Reprint AMF Warszawa 2005

69 In fact two, as the third was from the 21st Strike Squadron which he piloted with a pilot from the 7th FS serving as his observer.

70 It stood up on February 14, 1919 in Poznań. Being organized and first led by Rtm. Plt. Tadeusz Grochowski, it was equipped with the Fokker D.VII, Albatros D.III, Halberstadt CL II and CL IV. On April 2, 1919, it was deployed to Wielkopolska area of operations with Por. Pil. Edmund Norwid-Kudło in charge. It operated from Klenka near Nowe Miasto flying reconnaissance and propaganda sorties.

71 Originally, recognition marking was also painted on the bottom surface of the upper wing.

72 Some authors claim it was khaki.

73 In 1995 Dan-San Abbot in his article wrote about a three-color painting of the Albatros D.II upper surfaces. He based his assumption on a British report "Notes on German brought down in our lines – G42" signed on June 10, 1917, by Brig. Gen. R. Brooke-Popham.

74 The original description was "mixture of pale Brunswick green and white".

75 Dark Venetian red.

76 Olive green.

77 Available sources also define it as "German violet".

78 In English sources defined as 'lozenge', in German as 'lozengestarnstoff'.

79 Central Acceptance Committee.

80 After Technische Dedingingen für Flugzeuge. Auflage oktober 1917. Wien 1917.

81 A staging depot releasing all aircraft assigned to Fliks.

82 The starboard insignia was mirrored on the port side – it was a practice exercised on all Flik 3/J fighters.

83 Available pictures of the 13th FS's aircraft prove they all sported emblems.

84 The rest of the inscription is blocked by the standing soldier.

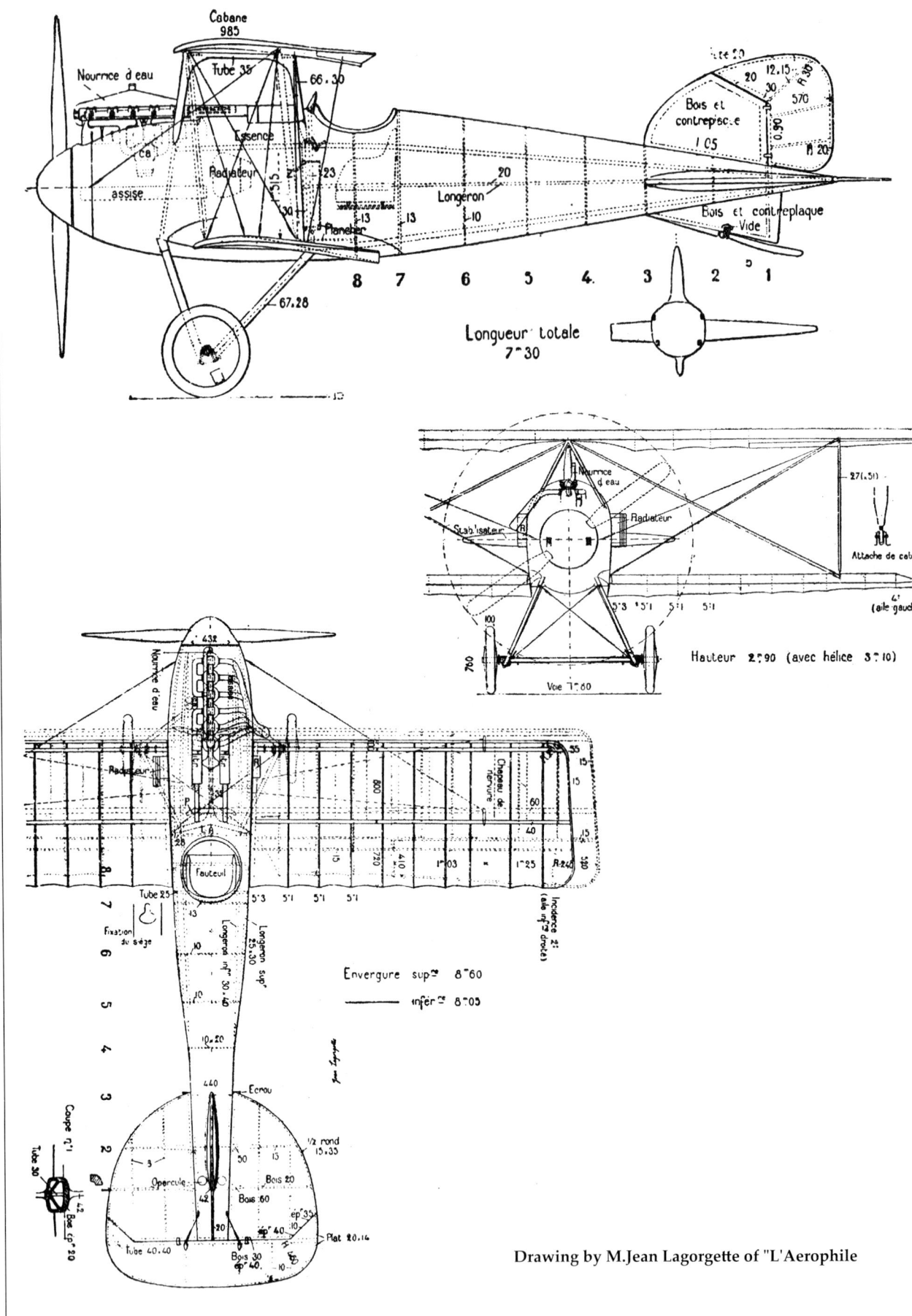

Drawing by M.Jean Lagorgette of "L'Aerophile

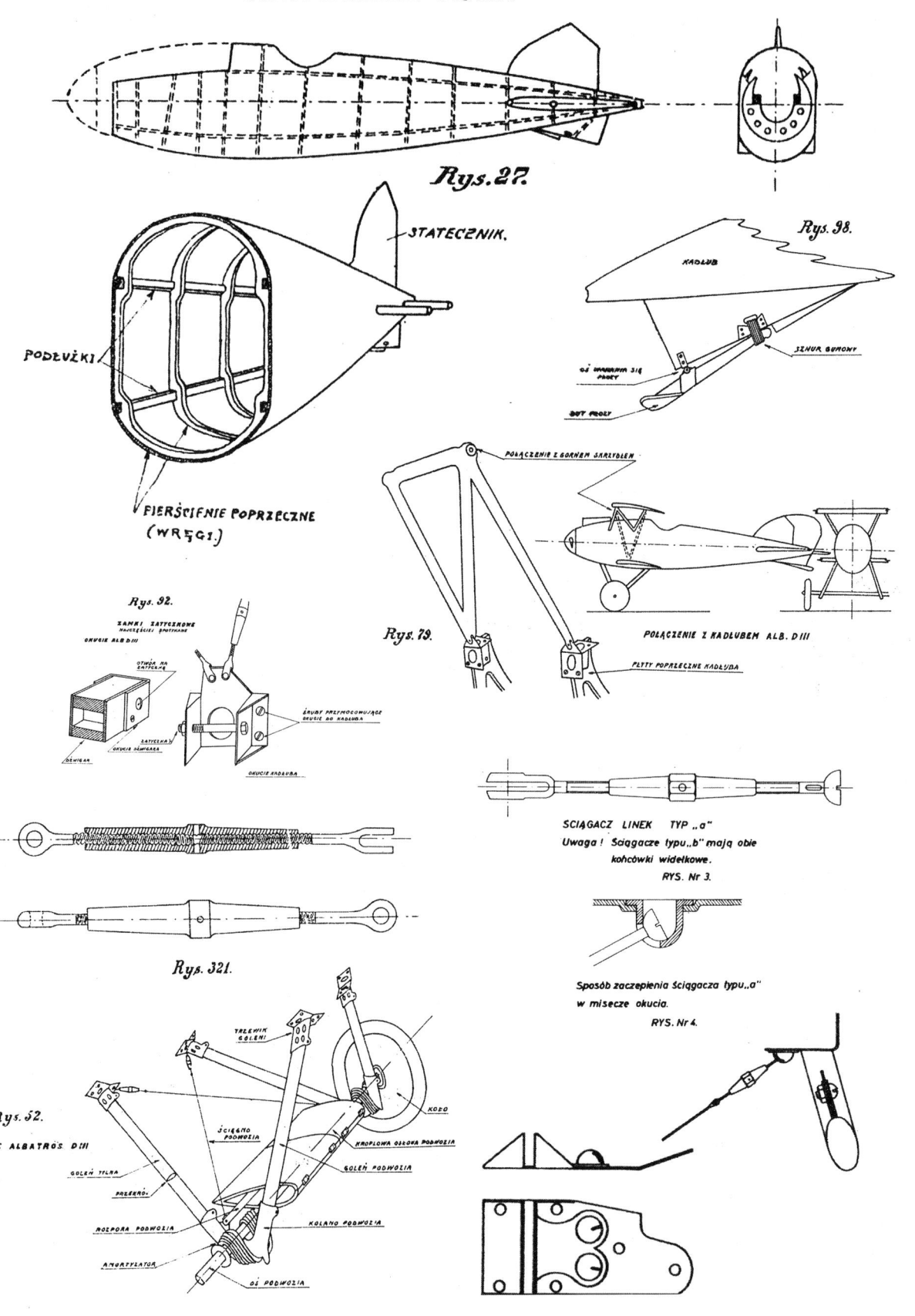

Kadłub Albatros D III.

Rys. 27.

STATECZNIK.

Rys. 98.

KADŁUB

PODŁUŻKI

PIERŚCIENIE POPRZECZNE
(WRĘGI.)

Rys. 92.

Rys. 79.

POŁĄCZENIE Z KADŁUBEM ALB. D III

SCIĄGACZ LINEK TYP „a"
Uwaga! Ściągacze typu „b" mają obie
końcówki widełkowe.
RYS. Nr 3.

Rys. 321.

Sposób zaczepienia Ściągacza typu „a"
w misecze okucia.
RYS. Nr 4.

Rys. 52.
PODWOZIE ALBATROS D III

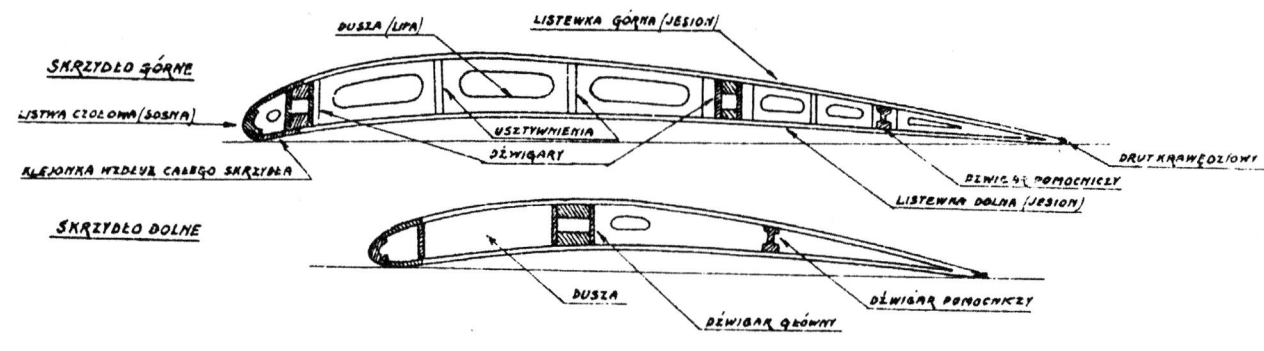

ŻEBERKO ALBATROSA D Ⅲ

SKRZYDŁO GÓRNE

DUSZA (LIPA)   LISTEWKA GÓRNA (JESION)

LISTWA CZOŁOWA (SOSNA)

USZTYWNIENIA

DŻWIGARY

KLEJONKA WZDŁUŻ CAŁEGO SKRZYDŁA

DRUT KRAWĘDZIOWY

DŻWIG 4; POMOCNICZY

LISTEWKA DOLNA (JESION)

SKRZYDŁO DOLNE

DUSZA

DŻWIGAR GŁÓWNY

DŻWIGAR POMOCNICZY

Rys. 286.

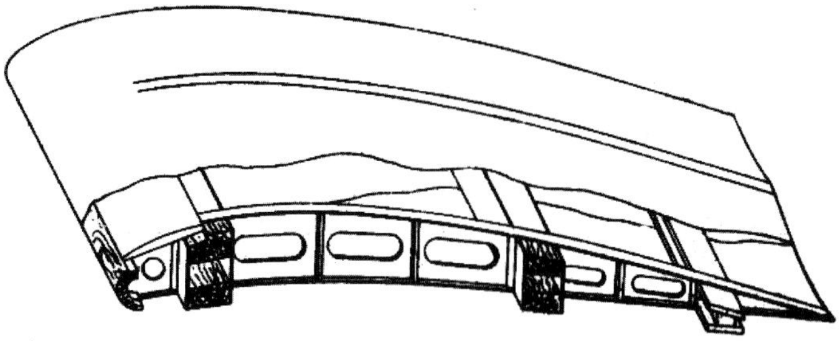

Rys. 146.

STEROWNICA ALBATROS D.III.

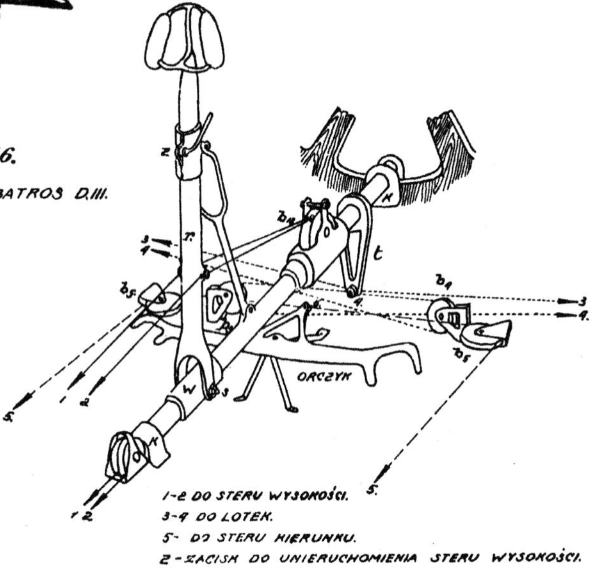

ORCZYK

1-2 DO STERU WYSOKOŚCI.
3-4 DO LOTEK.
5 - DO STERU KIERUNKU.
2 - ZACISK DO UNIERUCHOMIENIA STERU WYSOKOŚCI.

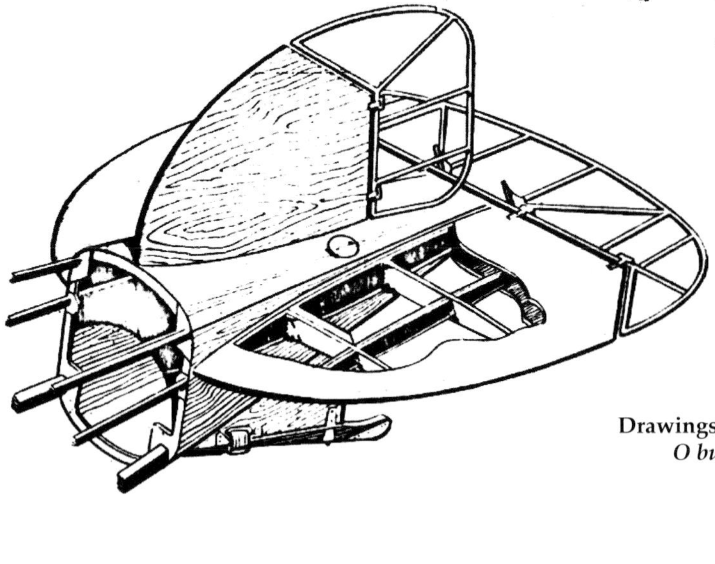

Drawings from book written by Zych Płodowski,
O budowie płatowców, Warszawa 1925

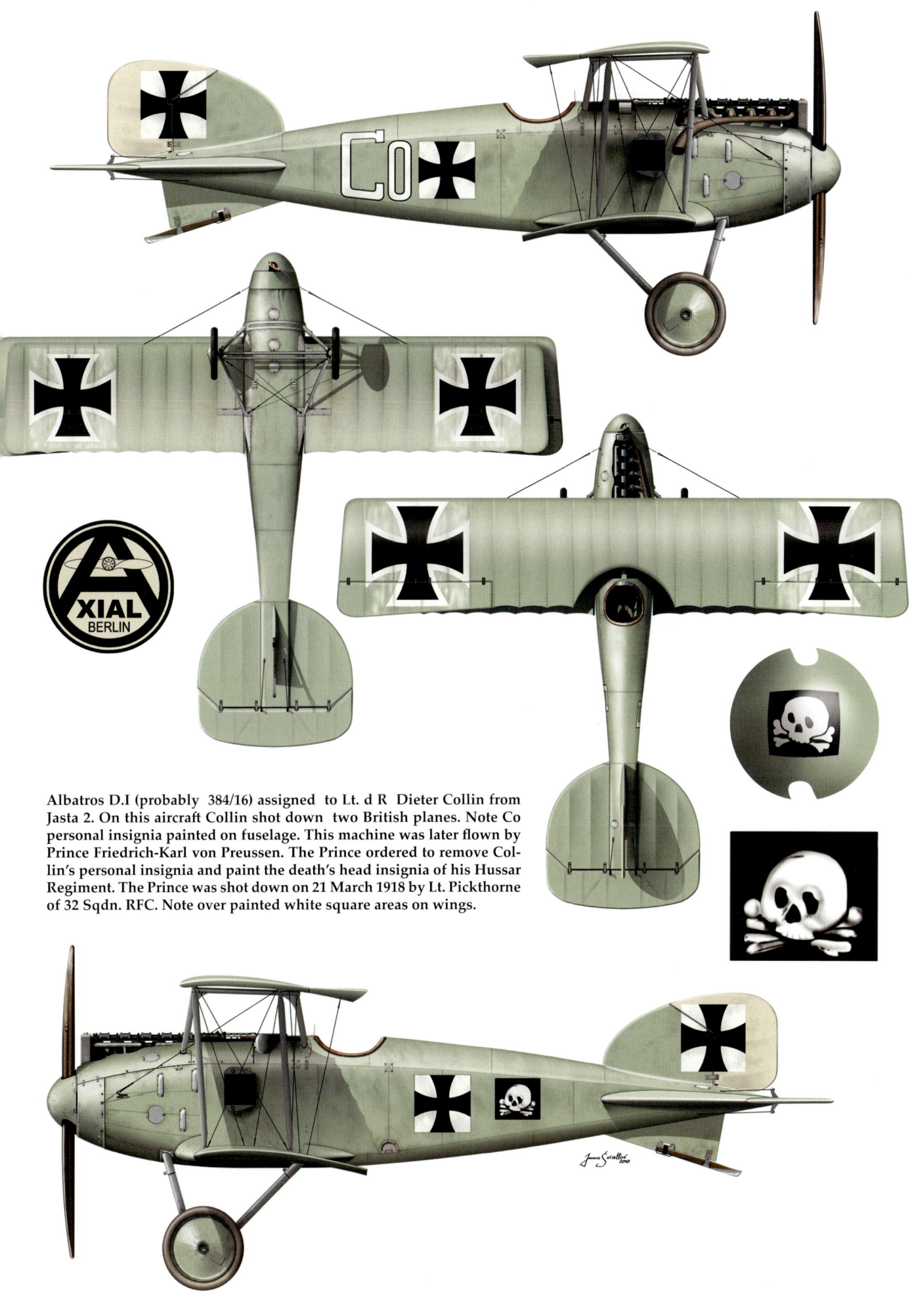

Albatros D.I (probably 384/16) assigned to Lt. d R Dieter Collin from Jasta 2. On this aircraft Collin shot down two British planes. Note Co personal insignia painted on fuselage. This machine was later flown by Prince Friedrich-Karl von Preussen. The Prince ordered to remove Collin's personal insignia and paint the death's head insignia of his Hussar Regiment. The Prince was shot down on 21 March 1918 by Lt. Pickthorne of 32 Sqdn. RFC. Note over painted white square areas on wings.

AXIAL BERLIN

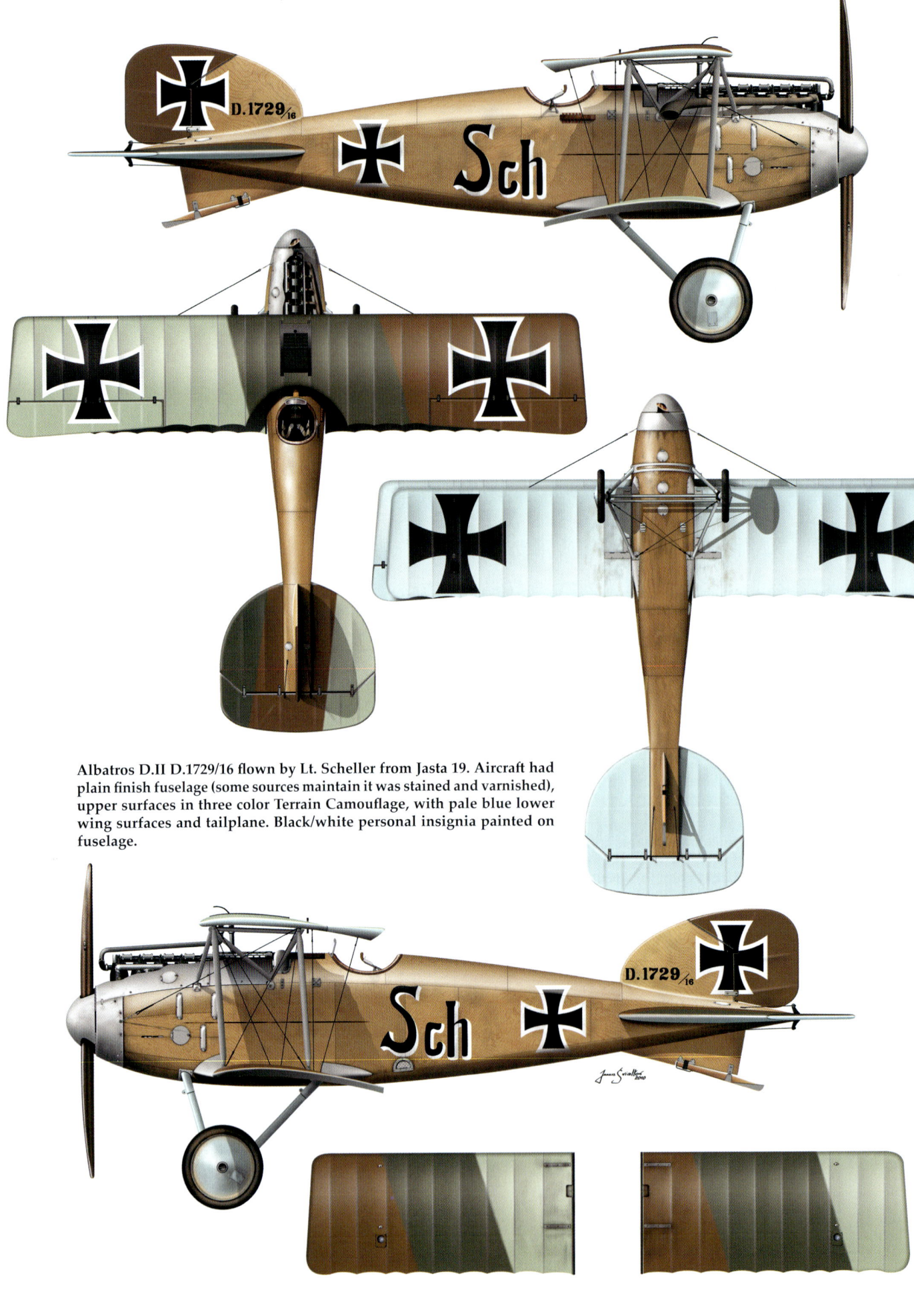

Albatros D.II D.1729/16 flown by Lt. Scheller from Jasta 19. Aircraft had plain finish fuselage (some sources maintain it was stained and varnished), upper surfaces in three color Terrain Camouflage, with pale blue lower wing surfaces and tailplane. Black/white personal insignia painted on fuselage.

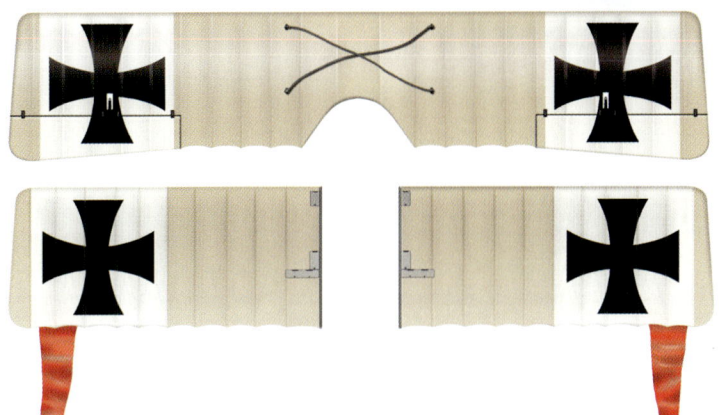

Prototype of Albatros W4, marine number 747 painted black on plain finish (possibly stained) fuselage, clear doped flying and control surfaces with all struts, engine panels and spinner grey-green. Floats was probably painted grey, Zeebrugge June 1916. This aircraft was written off on April 30 1917.

Albatros W4 marine number 1498 from German Navy Sea Group – Turkey 1917. Aircraft in full camouflage introduced on 3 April 1917 by See-Flugzeug Versuchs Kommando. All upper surfaces in 30 cm hexagons in three colors: grey-blue, grey-violet and grey-brown; all side surfaces and struts in grey blue, bottom of the fuselage in light grey, clear doped fabric under wings and tailplane.

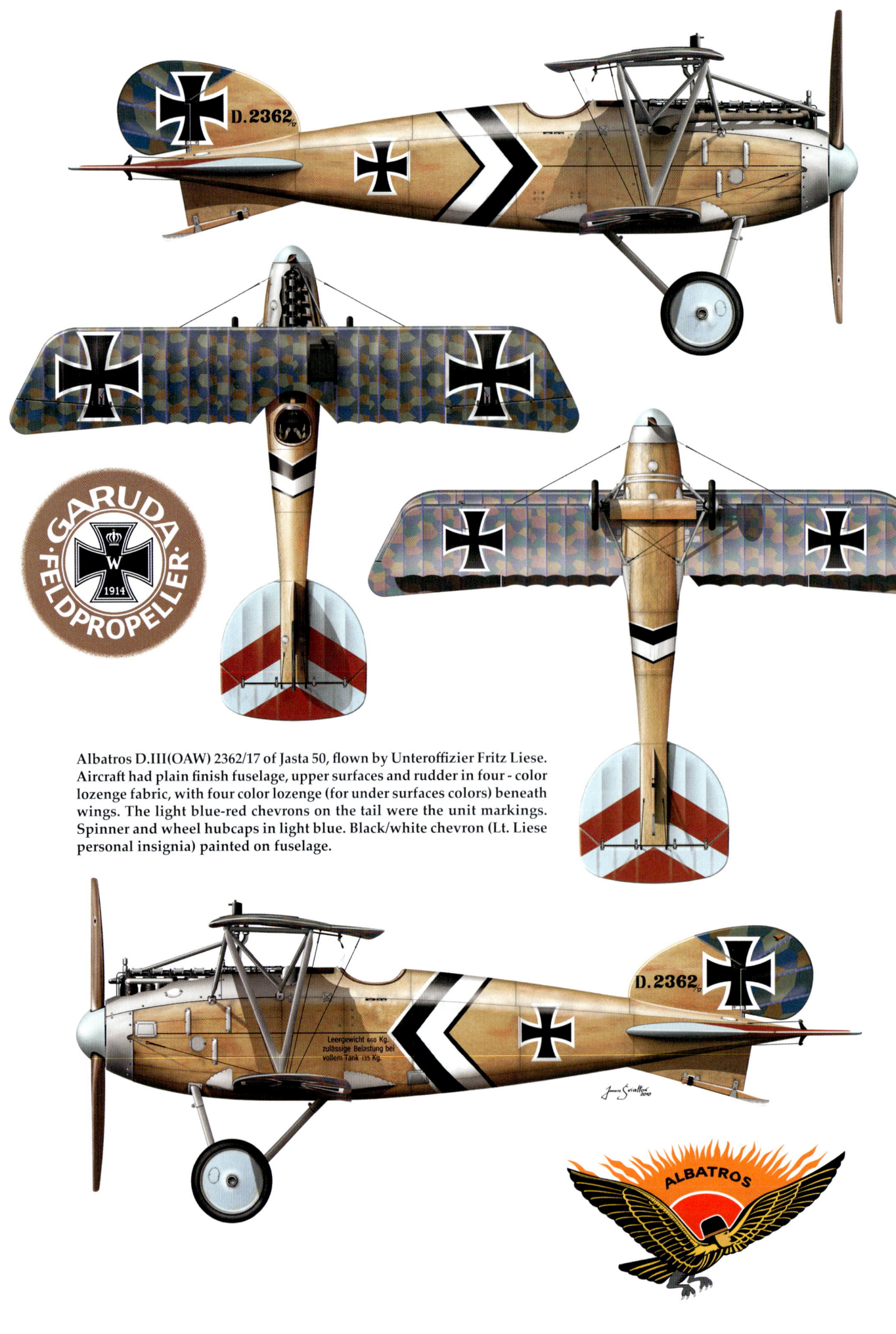

Albatros D.III(OAW) 2362/17 of Jasta 50, flown by Unteroffizier Fritz Liese.
Aircraft had plain finish fuselage, upper surfaces and rudder in four - color
lozenge fabric, with four color lozenge (for under surfaces colors) beneath
wings. The light blue-red chevrons on the tail were the unit markings.
Spinner and wheel hubcaps in light blue. Black/white chevron (Lt. Liese
personal insignia) painted on fuselage.

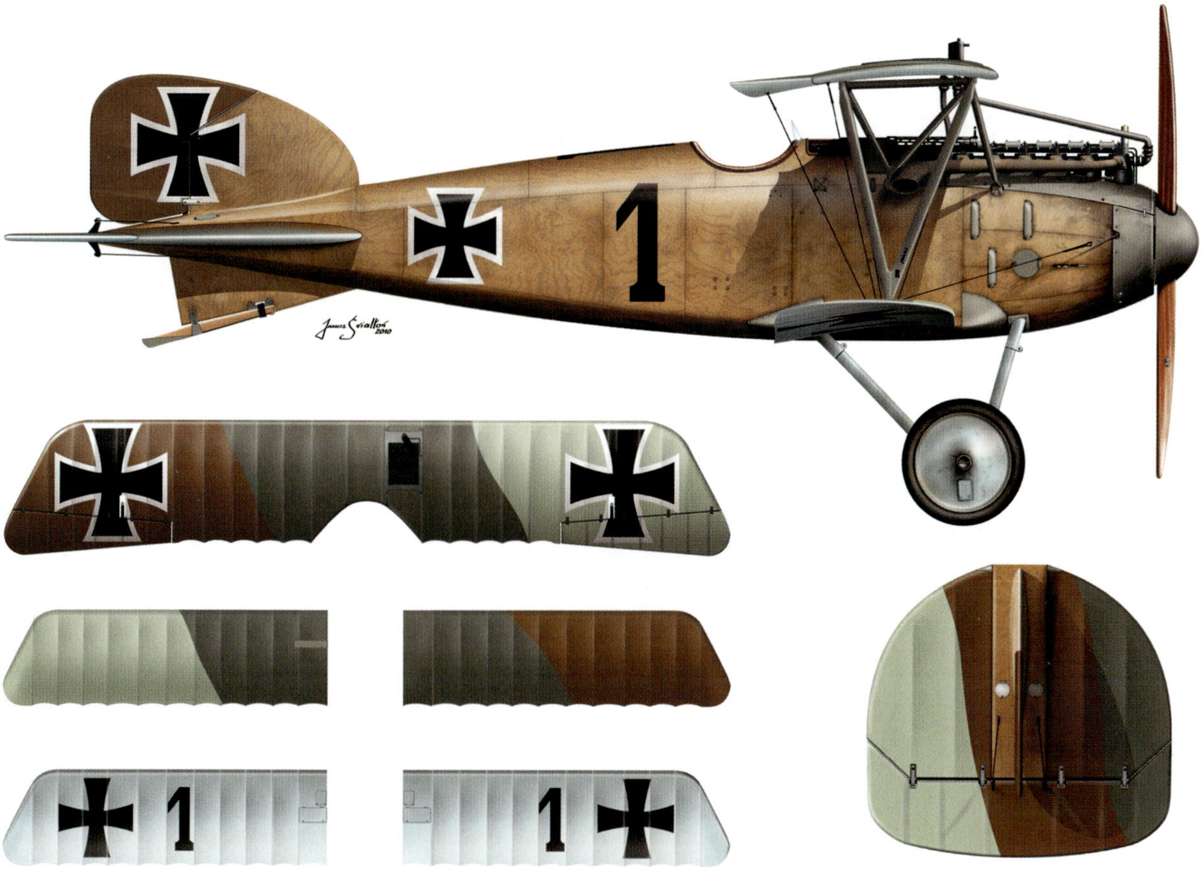

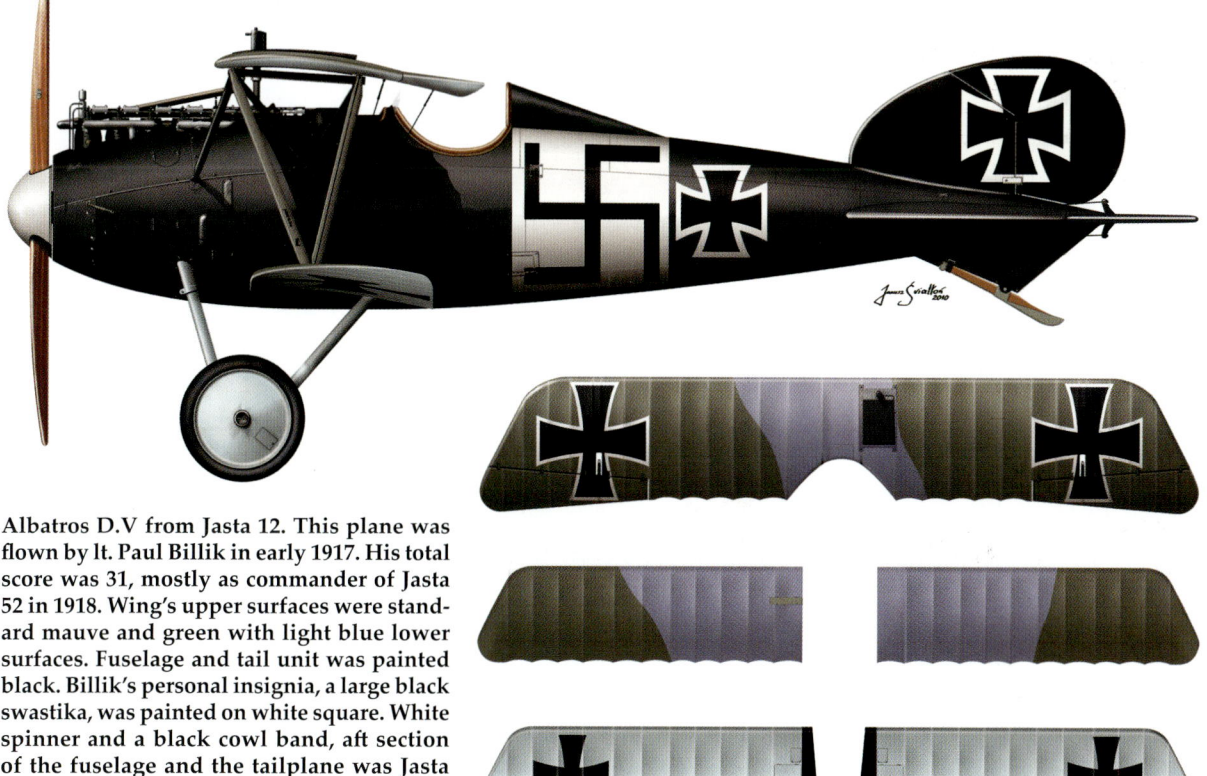

An Albatros D.III from Jasta 29. This aircraft was from the third and last production batch ordered in March 1917 and built at Johannistahl Albatros Factory. Upper surfaces of wings and tailplane were painted in three color terrain scheme. Note the usual German habit of repeating the aircraft number painted in black on both sides of fuselage and on the spine, probably painted on under surfaces of lower wings and fuselage.

Albatros D.V from Jasta 12. This plane was flown by lt. Paul Billik in early 1917. His total score was 31, mostly as commander of Jasta 52 in 1918. Wing's upper surfaces were standard mauve and green with light blue lower surfaces. Fuselage and tail unit was painted black. Billik's personal insignia, a large black swastika, was painted on white square. White spinner and a black cowl band, aft section of the fuselage and the tailplane was Jasta 12 markings. Remaining areas on fuselage painted black are Billik's personal color.

Albatros D.Va serial unknown of Oblt. Heinrich Gontermann from Jasta 15. Boncourt, autumn 1917. Gonterman's Albatros had a field-applied dark green dapple over silver-grey. Metal panels, struts and wheel hubs were silver-grey. Red band between cockpit and national insignia on the fuselage were Gonterman's personal markings. Note streamers in red-white-black colors affixed to the tailplane. Gonterman was the second top-scoring balloon ace with 17 kills (total sore 39).

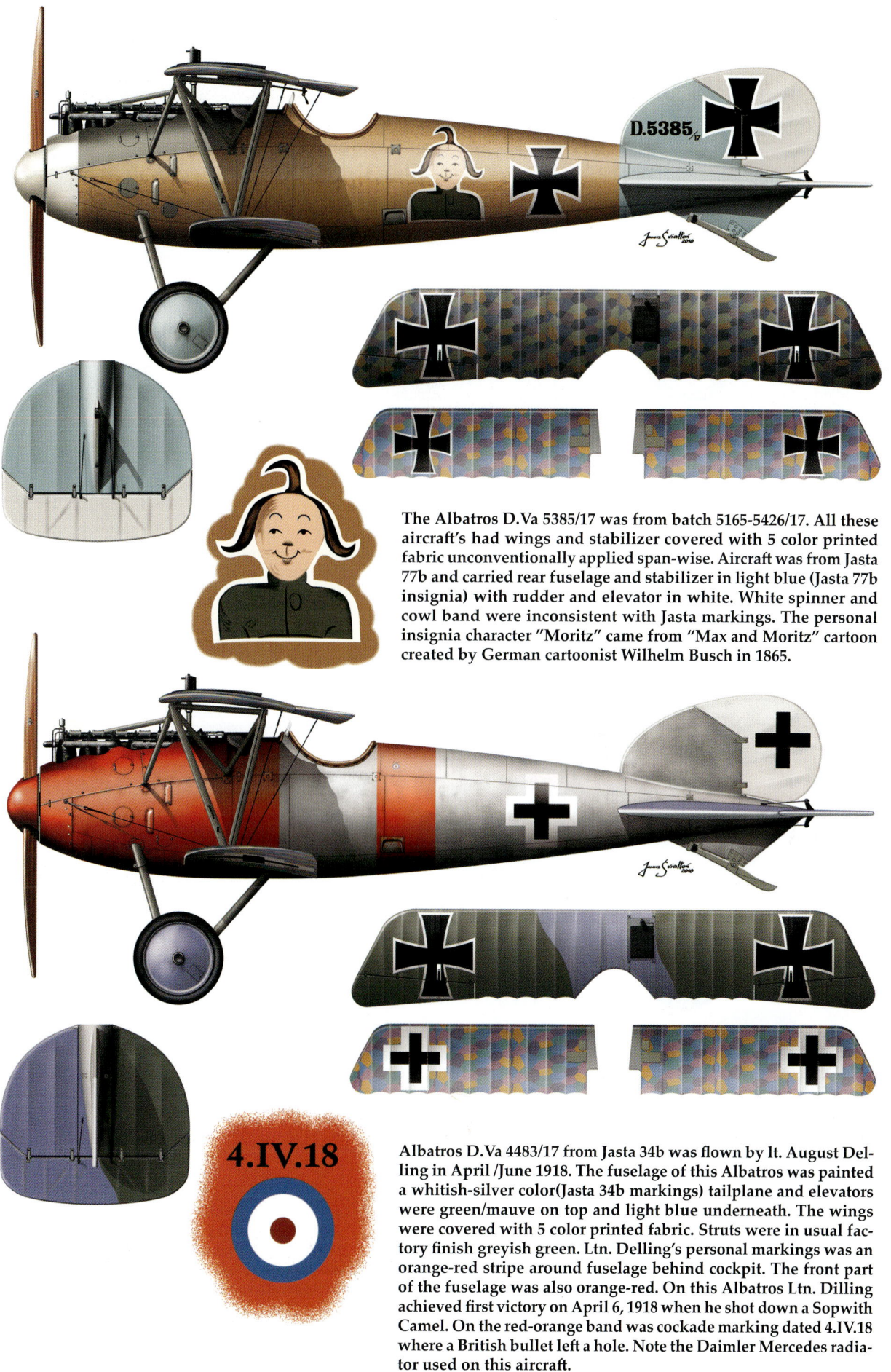

The Albatros D.Va 5385/17 was from batch 5165-5426/17. All these aircraft's had wings and stabilizer covered with 5 color printed fabric unconventionally applied span-wise. Aircraft was from Jasta 77b and carried rear fuselage and stabilizer in light blue (Jasta 77b insignia) with rudder and elevator in white. White spinner and cowl band were inconsistent with Jasta markings. The personal insignia character "Moritz" came from "Max and Moritz" cartoon created by German cartoonist Wilhelm Busch in 1865.

Albatros D.Va 4483/17 from Jasta 34b was flown by lt. August Delling in April /June 1918. The fuselage of this Albatros was painted a whitish-silver color(Jasta 34b markings) tailplane and elevators were green/mauve on top and light blue underneath. The wings were covered with 5 color printed fabric. Struts were in usual factory finish greyish green. Ltn. Delling's personal markings was an orange-red stripe around fuselage behind cockpit. The front part of the fuselage was also orange-red. On this Albatros Ltn. Dilling achieved first victory on April 6, 1918 when he shot down a Sopwith Camel. On the red-orange band was cockade marking dated 4.IV.18 where a British bullet left a hole. Note the Daimler Mercedes radiator used on this aircraft.

Albatros D.III(Oef) 253. xxx series from the 13th Eskadra Myśliwska (Fighter Squadron). Aircraft carried a very interesting artwork of Leda playing with swan - transformed Zeus. Aircraft had plain finish and carried the 13th Fighter Squadron insignia.

Albatros D.III(Oef) 253.218 from the 7th Eskadra Myśliwska (Fighting Squadron). This aircraft belonged to kpt. Meriam Cooper. Albatros had upper surfaces and rudder covered with Austro-Hungarian printed fabric. Fuselage was also painted in dark green. Numeral "5" repeated on upper and lower surfaces of wings and fuselage sides. Red nose markings indicate the Kościuszko Flight. Kiev, May 1920. This aircraft was burned by Polish personnel at Berdyczów in June 7th 1920.